Beaded Amulet Purses™

Select Bibliography

Beads, Beads, Beads. Sparks, NV: Taurus Publications, 1979.

Blakelock, Virginia. "Technical Hints for Bead Hunters," *European Bead Network, Perles INFO Perlen,* Berlin, Germany: Number 3, Autumn/Winter 1993, pp. 35-38.

Blakelock, Virginia. "Those Bad, Bad Beads," Wilsonville, Oregon, 1988.

Goodhue, Horace R. *Indian Bead-weaving Patterns.* St. Paul, MN: Bead-Craft, 1989.

Grainger, Barbara L. *Peyote at Last!* Oregon City, OR: Barbara L. Grainger, 1993.

Johnson, William H. "Things to Wear," *Needlecraft.* St. Paul, MN: Webb Book Publishing Company, 1942.

Porcelain Tile-craft Mats. New York, NY: Walco Toy Company, Inc., 1960.

Sako, Takako. *Bead Weaving.* Tokyo, Japan: NHK, 1992.

Short, Eirian. *Introducing Macramé.* Greenwich, CT: Fawcett Publications, Inc., 1970.

"Surface Finishes," *The Bead Lover's Bead Catalog.* Wilsonville, OR: Universal Synergetics, 1993.

Wells, Carol Wilcox. *Peyote Primer.* Crystal Lake, IL: Carol Wilcox Wells, 1992.

Wells, Carol Wilcox. "The Making of a Beaded Amulet Bag" (unpublished manuscript). Asheville, NC, 1994.

Revised Second Edition

©Copyright 1994, Revised Second Edition 1995, Nicolette Stessin

"Amulet Purses" is a trademark of Nicolette Stessin, registration pending.

All rights reserved under Pan American and International Copyright Conventions.

ISBN #0-9641865-0-0

Published in the United States by:
Beadworld Publishing
PO Box 99582
Seattle, WA 98199

Acknowledgments

First and foremost, I must thank the artists for their generosity in allowing us to photograph and include their purses in this book. The artists whose work became projects were especially helpful. We found that all the project artists are also beadwork teachers and are especially adept at explaining confusing material.

I particularly wish to thank Nancy Male for suggesting dotting the first bead of each row in tubular peyote graphs. Carol Wilcox Wells explained the turns in odd-count flat peyote stitch and suggested doing the first three rows of peyote stitch as a surrogate start and beginning the actual desired beading with the fourth row. Carol Perrenoud taught us the use of paper roll tubes as supports in the tubular off-loom stitches. M. Katsuoka, owner of the Miyuki Shoji Co., Ltd. of Japan, provided a detailed description of the loomed project purse. Genevieve Kreie suggested using size 14° seed beads in the reductions in the flat bottom basket purse. And David Chatt taught a private lesson in which he patiently answered many of my questions concerning the single-needle, right-angle weave.

The handmade background papers used in the photographs were supplied by, de Medici•Ming, Fine Paper of Seattle. The purse photographed for Project Two, Liquid Glass was made by Genevieve Kreie. The purses photographed for Projects Four and Seven, The Basket Bag and Damask (respectively) were made by Alice Scherer. The photograph of Lynne Irelan and Nancy Male was taken by Alice Scherer. I also wish to thank Alice for soliciting the participation of the Miyuki Shoji Co., Ltd. of Japan.

As this project bogged down, it was a gift to discover the help I needed was within the circle of people I already knew. Karla Englehardt, Mardie Rhodes, Genevieve Kreie, Larry Stessin and Harvey Bergman pulled me out of the morass with intelligence and grace — not to mention long hours. Karla Englehardt's name belongs next mine on the cover. As the credits make clear, hers is the creative energy in the superb illustrations and overall design of this book. I wish to reiterate that this book has been a team effort.

Organizing this effort took me through a lot of unfamiliar territory. My eight-year old daughter, Maya, and my husband, Larry, were both wonderfully encouraging and patient — particularly when I got grumpy. Many thanks also go to my friend Robin Hain who encouraged me to speak in my own voice.

Special thanks go to the instruction testers whose suggestions have made *Beaded Amulet Purses* so much better: Diane Amick, Marian Cave, Barbara Grainger, Lynne Irelan, Genevieve Kreie, Yvonne Ringle and Julie Selman. Genevieve Kreie tested and retested six of the purses and made numerous other samples which helped me understand the confusing material.

Author
Nicolette Stessin

Art Director
Karla Englehardt

Editor
Mardie Rhodes

Color Photographers
Larry Stessin
Harvey Bergman

Illustrator
Karla Englehardt

Graphic Designer
Karla Englehardt

Beadwork Advisor
Genevieve Kreie

**Early
Instructional Text
& Illustration Drafts**
Alice Scherer

Introduction

Across time women have always leaned toward the earth to gather rice, beans, flowers, berries and seeds. I share with my ancestors that same need to search for bright, small objects. My eye is so attracted to beads, those little spheres of color, that I've come to believe it's genetic. Today, my 20th century lifestyle has neither the time nor the necessity to satisfy my primal urge to gather food. I gather beads.

When I opened Beadworld, I was afraid my beloved beads would lose their appeal as I worked with them all day, every day. Instead, I've learned to appreciate many other beads. My customers are a constant source of inspiration and information. They've showed me how quickly novice beaders become adventurous artists. In fact, seeing their wonderful creations taught me a new appreciation for a bead that never spoke to me before — the common seed bead. These surprisingly simple beads are being used to create some of today's most sophisticated pieces.

Of all the beadwork I've seen, I kept coming back to these amulet purses. I never could find instructions for them. Thus, *Beaded Amulet Purses* was born. Some of the most innovative bead artists generously agreed to share their creations and techniques.

These artists clearly understand there are no hard and fast rules for designing with beads. Although the instructions in this book are quite specific, the variations are limitless. I hope this book is ultimately only a starting point. Since it is unlikely you will find all the specific beads used in these bags, substitute another one you love. This really is an opportunity!

I've noticed that people intuitively know the colors and shapes that look good on them. Remember that design and color choice are both a matter of personal taste. Often the best designs are born when we let go of the rules and tap unexpected sources of inspiration. Create a personal notebook of design. You'll turn to it again and again. When you find beads you love, trust that you'll find a way to use them. This is your time, your vision, your adventure. No one can do it better. Trust yourself!

As all of us gather and work with beads, we share a creative process which is unchanged since the dawn of personal expression. Beads thread us through time with our ancient ancestors, linking our vision of beauty. Can there be a better connection?

— Nicolette Stessin

I lovingly dedicate this book to my parents...I miss them.

The Beadworld Publishing Team:

Karla Englehardt, top
Mardie Rhodes, left
Genevieve Kreie, right
Nicolette Stessin, bottom

How To Use This Book

After choosing a project, first read the instructions and the recommended pages from the appendices for the specific technical information to make that amulet purse. Please make samples if you are unfamiliar with the nuances of a beading stitch. Spending the time now will almost certainly save a lot of time and frustration later and improve the quality of your work. Besides — the more comfortable you are with the beading process, the more serendipitous design opportunities you'll discover to individualize even your first purse. You are welcome to photocopy and color the bead graphs for your own use.

There are more than 90 figures throughout the book to help explain the techniques used in the seven projects. In each figure, the dotted and shaded beads correspond with the dotted and shaded beads in each bead graph. In addition, the black-line beads illustrate the beads being worked; the gray-line beads are the ones already added. The thread gaps between the beads are for clarity only and do not show in the finished work.

Regardless of which project you choose, read the following section on beading supplies and Appendix B, "Threads, Knots and Bead Graphs". To a certain degree, we've numbered the projects based on difficulty. Projects Six and Seven are particularly advanced.

Beading Supplies and Other Aids

These Beaded Amulet Purses require little or no special equipment.

- Glass seed beads
- Thread
- Needles
- Small scissors
- Beeswax
- Thin, strong glue
- A small pair of flat nose pliers
- A loom for Project Five
- Optional — a set of small jewelry files, called broaches.

Beads

Sizes

Glass seed beads are sized from 1° to 24°, the higher the number, the smaller the bead. Typical sizes are 1°, 5°, 6°, 8°, 9°, 10°, 11°, 12°, 13°, 14°, 15°, 16°, 18°, 20°, 22° and 24°. However, the actual dimension of a designated size may vary depending on the manufacturer or the era. Size 11° has the greatest range of colors and is the most readily available. Today, bead manufacturers concentrate on making sizes 6° through 14°. Seed beads smaller than a 14° are not easy to find. Addicted beaders routinely spend years of dedicated gathering to collect a varied palette of colors in the very small sizes. These projects will require using the same size seed bead in at least the main body of the purse. It takes a lot of experience to be able to mix bead sizes within the bead-weaving.

Cut Beads

Cut seed beads are faceted so they can reflect more light and, therefore, shimmer. Currently, they are produced as either a two-cut, hex-cut, three-cut or charlotte. Two-cut beads are seed beads cut from square glass cane, almost the same length as a size 1/2 bugle. Hex-cut seed beads are six-sided cylindrical size 15° Japanese beads with a large hole. These light-weight beads are a favorite with earring makers. Three-cut seed beads are faceted seed beads. The standard shape seed beads are strung on a wire and then shaped into a faceted bead using a grindstone. Charlottes, sometimes called "true cuts" are a size 13° Czech seed bead with one hand-cut facet. These are the wonderful beads that seems to wink in native american beadwork.

Delicas

The Japanese have recently developed a new smooth cylindrical seed bead, the delica and "antique" bead, known in the United States as "delicious" beads. These cylindrical beads are almost a cube and most nearly approximate a size 12° seed bead. Delicas are rapidly gaining favor for their uniform size, unusual colors and large holes.

Bugle Beads

Bugle beads are longer sections of the same drawn glass tubing cut to make seed beads. Bugle beads are often snapped off to length and sometimes have ragged and sharp ends. This can cut your threads, so always check each bead. Sometimes, ragged bugles can be filed with a flat jewelry file. Bugles come in sizes 1/2 through 35. They are numbered sizes 1/2, 1, 2, 3, 4, 5 and then jump to 15, 20, 25, 30 and 35. The higher the number, the longer the bugle. Sizes 2, 3 and 5 are the most commonly used and readily available. A size 11° seed bead is the closest in diameter to a bugle.

Uniformity & Color

Glass seed beads are manufactured in the Czech Republic, Japan, India, France, Taiwan, China and until recently, Italy. The quality of these beads can vary widely. You will need to check for consistency in overall size and in the size of the bead hole within the same hank or container of beads. Furthermore, it is important to check the durability of the bead's color.

Work Tip: *To check for misshapen beads; line one or more shallow dishes with a light colored material and some with a dark colored material. We recommend small stackable water color trays, available at art supply stores. Lined with suede or very thin wale corduroy. Put a single layer of dark colored beads in the dishes with the light material and light colored beads in the dishes with the dark material. As you are picking up beads to incorporate in the woven beadwork, the irregular beads will be easier to spot against a contrasting background color.*

Work Tip: *If you are still unsure of a bead's uniformity, take a tip from pearl stringers. Place several beads on a needle and roll the beads up and down against a finger. If the hole in a bead is not centered, the bead will wobble as it rolls up and down your finger.*

Glass seed beads are made from opaque, transparent, opalescent, satin and greasy glass. The colors of these types of glass are inherently permanent. However, because we want colors which are impossible, difficult or expensive to make, glass seed beads are often colored.

Transparent seed beads are sometimes colored by lining the hole with silver or paint. Color-lined beads are usually less risky because once they are incorporated into your beadwork, they don't get a lot of wear. Transparent beads are surface dyed and seem to fade easily, especially the bright pinks. Opaque beads are colored by applying a surface coating, such as an iris, ceylon, galvanized or metallic finish. All treated seed beads need to be examined for quality. Many are durable, but some are not colorfast or do scratch easily. Do not hesitate to ask your bead supplier if a bead's color will fade or rub off.

Work tip: *To test for permanence or durability, dip a sample of beads into bleach, alcohol or acetone (some fingernail polish removers). Leave the beads in the solution for at least an hour. Always test unfamiliar fuschias, bright pinks and purples.*

If a bead surface is not durable and you feel you must use it anyway, you can extend the life of the coating by sealing the bead with a spray fixative. We recommend Krylon, a clear acrylic fixative, available from art supply stores. All galvanized beads will scratch and we recommend sealing with a fixative. If a bead scratches easily, no amount of fixative will make it a good choice.

Work tip: *To use Krylon, test a small sample of beads first. Then place a single layer of beads in a shallow, disposable container. Shake the container while spraying the beads with a light coating. Continue shaking the beads for a few minutes until they are dry. This prevents the beads from lying in the wet fixative and drying with an uneven application of sealer. We recommend several light coats rather than one or two thicker applications. Krylon is not permanent but does afford some protection.*

Work tip: *You can matte the shiny surface of transparent and opaque glass beads by dipping them for sixty seconds in a hydrofluoric acid compound such as Jack Frost, by McKay International of Fairfield, New Jersey. This is a corrosive chemical which requires careful use. Treated beads will lose their finish when etched with Jack Frost, so only etch transparent or opaque beads. Using shiny and matte versions of the same bead gives a wonderful textural quality to a design.*

We recommend selecting all the beads for a project before you begin. Otherwise, you might complete the bead-weaving and not be able to find matching beads for the strap, fringe, etc. Glass is like yarn, the exact color will vary from dye lot to dye lot. Buy enough beads to complete your project.

Needles

Beading needles are specially made to pass through the small holes of seed beads. Unlike a sewing needle whose shaft flares out to accommodate a larger hole, the shaft of the beading needle is uniform along its entire length. Therefore, they have unusually small holes and can be difficult to thread. The number on the package corresponds to the size of the bead. Use a size 10 beading needle with size 10° seed beads. A size 12 beading needle for size 11° or 12° seed beads. A size 15 for the especially small size seed beads.

Japanese beading needles are one diameter only and the size refers to the length of the needle, not the thickness of the shaft. The higher the number, the longer the needle. They work well with a size 11° or larger seed bead and the delicas.

Bead looming will require a long needle. Otherwise, a shorter needle is a good choice because it easier to use and less likely to break. Size 10 milliner or quilting needles can be used for the off-loom techniques with size 11° or larger seed beads and the delicas. The size of needle will depend on the size of the beads and the number of passes of thread in each bead. All things being equal, use the largest needle that will do the job.

Threads

Nymo brand nylon thread is one of the most commonly available. It comes in sizes 000, 00, 0, A, B, C, D, E, F, FF, FFF. The sizing begins with size 000 as the thinnest through size FFF as the thickest. Size D is a good overall choice for these projects.

Kevlar is another thread employed by beaders. Used to weave a fabric for bullet-proof vests, this thread is very strong and thin. Ironically, it can cut itself when tied in a knot, therefore we recommend you organize your beadwork so there are no knots. It does fray easily. Use shorter lengths and beeswax it well.

Rice's Waxed Silamide or Gudebrod's Polymide can also be used for size 8-11° seed beads. Both are available from fabric stores.

Work tip: *If you cannot find an appropriate color of thread, you can color white Nymo with a permanent fabric marker. Place a length of thread on some scrap paper, apply the edge of the marker to one end and pull the thread through the dye.*

Work tip: *After threading the needle, run the thread once or twice over a block of beeswax. This strengthens the thread, helps prevent fraying and inhibits unwanted knots.*

Work tip: *Keep a small pair of jewelry pliers on hand to pull a needle through a particularly tight bead. Hold the needle where it exits the bead, not at the point, and pull gently. As soon as the needle clears the bead, pull the thread through with your fingers. If possible, avoid this situation because the thread at the eye of the needle frays as you tug on it. The needle may also break.*

Bead Graph Paper & Templates

A variety of bead graph papers have come on the market in the last few years. Graph papers for loomed bead weaving, peyote stitch, herringbone weave, right-angle weave and netting stitches can help translate artwork to an accurately sized beadwork pattern. They are available in each of the stitches for sizes 10° to 24° seed beads.

Beading templates can make the process even easier. They are transparent plastic sheets with imprinted beadwork patterns. A template for the desired stitch and bead size is placed on top of your artwork and then color-copied. The result is a color copy of the artwork with a super-imposed graphic of the seed beads.

Lightweight Supports for Beading

For projects worked in the round — tubular peyote and tubular lattice netting — a light weight beading support is recommended. It's unlikely you'll be able to find something precisely the inner diameter of the first circle of beads. To make a custom-sized support, slit a cardboard paper towel tube or toilet paper tube, compress it with your hand and slide it into the circle of beads. Allow it to expand to fit the inner diameter of the circle. Tape the top and bottom of the tube together. Take the tube out of the circle of beads. Place packing tape along the full length of the seam. Slide the tube back into the circle and commence beading. This makes a very light support which isn't tiring to hold for long stretches of beading.

A final word. Most of us realize that we can be obsessive about beading. It is far too easy to let hour after hour go by without taking a break. Then, when we try to get up from our chair, we can barely move. My sister and I set the alarm on our oven for one hour. That makes us get up to turn it off. And usually, we are good about making a cup of coffee or walking around a little before beading again.

Project One
Heart Bag

Lynne Irelan and Nancy Male

Nancy Male and Lynn Irelan were inspired by bargello needlepoint patterns. Lynn graphed out the pattern within the tubular peyote stitch medium. Nancy applied her interest in color and the subtle shadings of color to realize the heart motif and the more subtle chevrons within the purse design. Lynn and Nancy usually spend a lot of time choosing the right rock or crystal to put in each of their bags.

Sections to be read before beginning:
- Tubular Peyote Stitch — Even-Count (page 46)
- Threads, Knots and Bead Graphs (page 52)
  - To begin tubular peyote stitch (page 53)
  - How to read even-count tubular peyote graphs (page 57)

Materials used:
- Size 11° seed beads:
  - Transparent pale blue
  - Silver-lined medium pink
  - Silver-lined emerald green
  - Silver-lined cobalt blue
- Strap:
  - Czech molded glass beads
  - Semi-precious stone chips:
    - malachite, lapis and peridot
- Small pendant

This project is a flattened tube with the bottom stitched together.

To begin. Start with the bottom right bead of the graph on page 11. String once and then again the 26 beads of the first two rows on the graph. These 52 beads constitute the first two rows of both the front and back of the bag.

Tie the beads into a circle leaving a four– to six–inch tail (figure 1). Allow a three-bead space between the knot and the beads. Otherwise, the first three rows will be too tight. This space is taken up when you do row three.

Figure 1

Place the circle of beads over a support. See Lightweight Supports for Beading (page 7). Make sure the beads to the left of the knot are the first beads on the bottom right of the graph. If not, the pattern will be backwards.

Working from right to left, take the needle back through the first bead on the graph. Then pick up the first dotted bead (figure 2 and graph) and pass the needle through bead number three. Continue to pick up and stitch the next 12 beads of row three as indicated on the graph. Pick-up and stitch this same pattern of 13 beads again to complete row three.

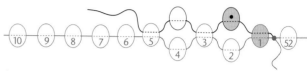

Figure 2

At the end of row three you must step-up to begin row four (figure 3). After picking up the last bead of row three (bead A), you will meet the first bead of row three (bead B). Take the needle through bead B and then through the dotted bead (bead C). Passing through both bead B and C is the step-up, and why the dotted bead always contains three threads. You're now ready to begin row four.

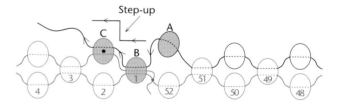

Figure 3

Note: The dotted beads on the graph represent the first bead of each new row.

To create the body of the purse, stitch all the rows on the graph, stepping up at the end of each row. From time-to-time, slide the woven beads down the support.

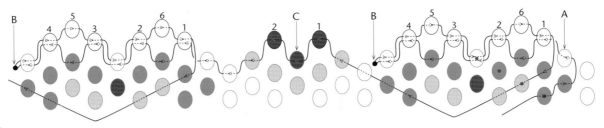

Figure 4

To outline the hearts at the top rim. Begin a new thread by zig-zagging through the beads below and to the right of any heart on the top. Bring the needle out through bead A and add beads one, two, three and four (figure 4). Half-hitch the working thread around the woven thread at B. Reverse direction and pick up beads five and six. Reverse direction again and bring the needle down through the beads in the body of the bag and over to the next half-heart. Add a bead on either side of C, the center bead. Repeat, until all the hearts and half-hearts are outlined.

To stitch the bottom closed. Remove the beaded tube from the support. Turn the beaded tube over, so the bottom of the purse is now facing up, ready to be closed. Align the half hearts at the top of the purse. With a new knotted thread, zig-zag to the last right bead of the bottom and pull the knot into a bead (hiding the knot). Nudge the two halves of the tube to one side or the other until the uppermost beads form a "zipper" (figure 5). Stitch back and forth between the front and back portions of the tube to close the bottom.

To add the pendant. To support the weight of the pendant, zig zag the needle through the woven beads with several half-hitches and exit bead D (figure 6). Pick up three seed beads. The third is bead E. String sufficient seed beads to allow the pendant to hang freely. Add the pendant and enough seed beads to come back to bead E with the pendant hanging in the center. Pass again through bead E and add beads four and five. Take the needle through several beads in the woven purse and half-hitch around a woven thread. For added strength, backtrack through beads five, four and E. Continue through the beads holding the pendant and then again through beads E, two and one. Zig-zag the thread into the woven beads with several more half-hitches.

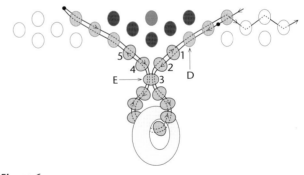

Figure 6

Figure 5. *The gray or white color of the beads is for clarity only and does not represent what you will see.*

To make the strap. Think of the strap as a necklace. Choose the seed beads and larger focal beads for the strap. Decide the ideal length and arrange the focal beads and seed beads into a symmetrical design (see photograph, page 8). Be sure to leave at least 20 inches of thread at each end of the strap. String on one or more focal beads. Pick up and thread enough seed beads to span the distance to the next focal bead. Continue in this fashion until all the beads of the first strand are strung.

With a second thread pass through the first focal bead(s). String enough seed beads to span the distance to the next focal bead. Take the needle through that focal bead, string more seed beads and so on, until you reach the last focal bead.

Using a surgeon's knot, tie both strands together against the first focal bead. Hold on to the other ends and hang the two strands down. Shift the beads until there are no spaces between any of the beads in the strands. Tie a second surgeon's knot snugly against the last focal bead at the other end.

Zig-zag all four tails through the woven beads of the purse. Since the strap will carry all the weight of the purse, tie several half-hitches with each tail.

Heart Bag

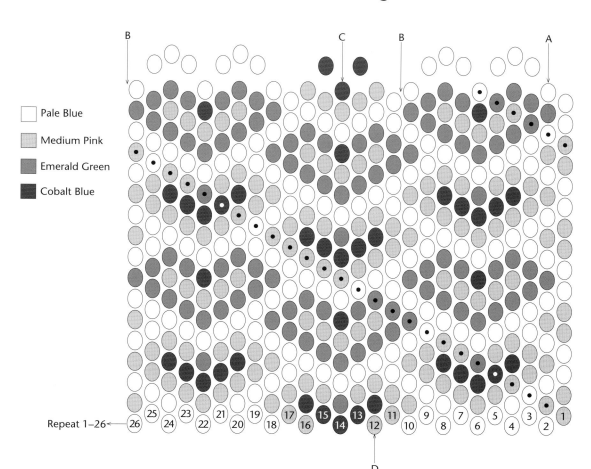

Pale Blue
Medium Pink
Emerald Green
Cobalt Blue

Repeat 1–26

Project Two
Liquid Glass

Wynter-rayne Matthews

Wynter-rayne Matthews believes beads have so many voices, "The finished design depends on who's playing with them." If we all started with the same beads, none of us would have the same end creation. She describes beads as ethereal and evocative. She never graphs out a pattern but works intuitively. If the design process bogs down, she lets the project rest and often dreams the solution. "Then it's my bag."

Sections to read before beginning:
- Flat Peyote Stitch — Odd-Count (page 44)
  - Decreasing at the sides (page 45)
- Fringe (page 51)
- Threads, Knots and Bead Graphs (page 52)
  - To begin flat peyote stitch (page 53)
  - How to read flat peyote stitch graphs (page 56)

Materials used:
- Miyuki delica seed beads. See the graph on page 15 for a color key.
- Beads for the pendant on the triangular flap.
- Twisted bugles for the fringe.
- Size 4 or 5 bugle beads to decorate the side seams of the bag.
- Assorted beads for the strap, including:
  - Austrian crystals, Czech molded glass beads, Japanese twisted bugles and delicas.

This bag is a classic envelope shape that is closed by sewing together the sides.

Note: The bright pink seed beads used in this purse, DB-422, will scratch with abrasion. See Work Tip (page 6) for how to spray fix beads with risky colors.

To bead the flat panel. Temporarily secure a stop bead to the end of the thread leaving a 4-inch tail. Pick up the 39 beads of rows one and two as indicated on the bottom of the graph (page 15). In order to center the geometric design of the purse, there are an odd number of beads in the base strand. Working from right to left, pick up the first bead of row three and pass the needle back through bead 38 of the base strand (figure 1). Pick up the next bead of row three, thread back through bead 36 and so on. Upon reaching the end of row three, there will be no place to put the last bead and make the turn to begin row four.

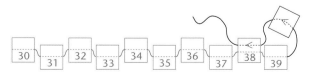

Figure 1

To hold the last bead in place and complete row three, do a figure eight threading pattern (figure 2). Pick up the last bead of row three and take the needle through bead one. Pass the needle back through bead two, down to the bead three, up to the second last bead of row three, back through bead two, then through bead one and finally around the outside edge and through the last bead of row three. You're now ready to begin row four.

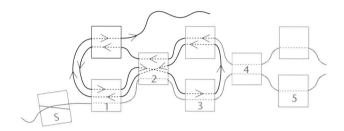

Figure 2

Upon completing row four, there will be a place to put the last bead and finish the turn. However, at the end of row five, you are again faced with no place for the last bead to complete the row. Only row three requires a figure eight threading pattern. From now on, half-hitch around the edge thread between the previous two rows (figure 3). In the rectangular portion of the graph, all odd numbered rows will require an adjustment to hold the last bead in place.

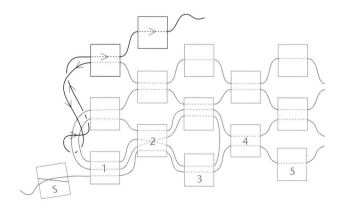

Figure 3

To make the triangular flap. After completing the last row of the rectangular portion of the work, begin reducing each side to create the flap. To reduce, stop one bead short at the beginning and end of each row, using half-hitches as indicated. (figure 4).

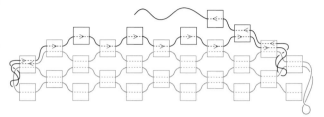

Figure 4. The illustration does not show all the beads of the rows.

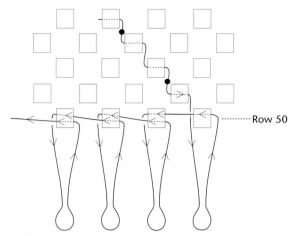

Row 50

Figure 5

Continue to reduce on each side of each row until only one bead is left. Do not clip the thread. String the pendant beads and then pass the needle back through all but the bottom bead. Zig-zag back into the woven beads and clip the thread.

To create the fringe. To find row 50, the fringe row, fold points A and C to meet points B and D (see graph on page 15). The beads of row 50 will be used to anchor the fringe. With the outside surface facing you, zig-zag a new thread with a few half-hitches through the body of the bag. Exit between the last and second to the last bead on the fold — row 50 (figure 5).

String:
- One bronze seed bead
- One bronze delica
- One gold delica
- One bronze delica
- One black twisted bugle
- One bronze seed bead
- One black delica
- One black crystal bead
- One black delica
- Five green delicas

To make a loop with the five green delicas, return the thread through the remaining beads of the fringe — beginning with the last black delica.

Be sure the fringe has no thread gaps and is pulled snugly against the woven beads Take the needle through the first two woven beads of row 50. String the second fringe and continue, creating fringes across the fold row. Upon reaching the opposite side, zig-zag the thread with a few half-hitches into the body of the bag and clip.

To close the purse. Fold points A and C up to meet points B and D to create the envelope (see graph on page 15). Zig-zag a new thread through the woven beads and exit through either bead B or D. Starting at the opening of the bag, stitch the sides together using half-hitches around the edge threads. At the top do a few extra half-hitches for extra strength. Repeat these steps to close the other side.

To make the strap. Think of the strap as a necklace. Decide the ideal length and design of the strap and arrange the beads accordingly. Use connector beads at regular and symmetrical intervals (see photograph, page 12).

Without attaching to the purse, string one strand of the strap. Leave at least a 20 inch tail of thread on each end. With a new length of thread pass through the first set of connector beads. Mimicking the first strand, pick up and string enough seed beads to span the distance to the next connector bead. Pass the thread through the connector bead. Continue stringing the second strand, converging through the connector beads.

Using a surgeon's knot, tie the two strands together at each end. Run the ends of the strap down each side seam of the bag, adding a few half-hitches from time to time. Align and stitch seed and bugle beads along each side seam to obscure the threads. See the photograph on page 12.

Liquid Glass

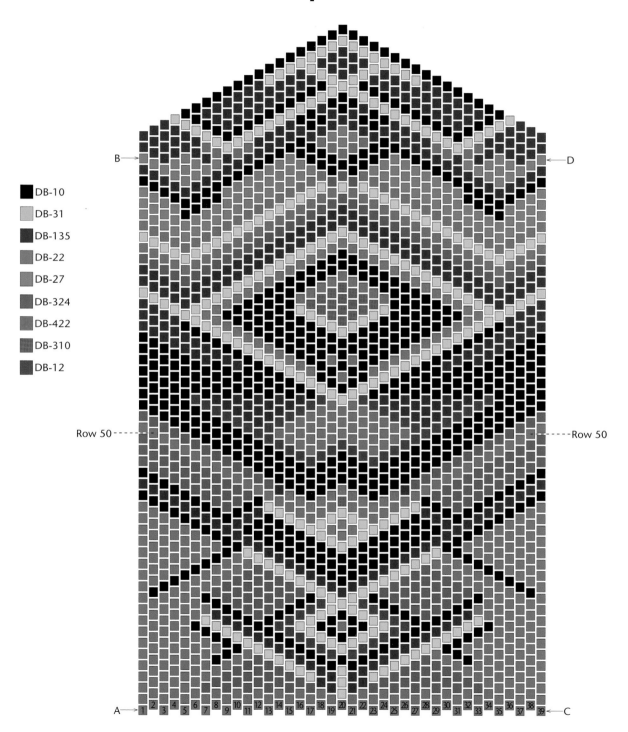

Project Three

Rain Forest Medicine Bag

Yvonne Ringle

Yvonne Ringle was drawn to beading by the creative color and texture possibilities afforded by the tiny seed bead. She also enjoys the soothing nature of adding one bead at a time and watching the pattern and color develop slowly.

Sections to be read before beginning:

• Tubular Lattice Netting (page 47)
• Fringe (page 51)
• Threads, Knots and Bead Graphs (page 52)
    • To begin tubular lattice netting (page 54)
    • How to read tubular lattice netting graphs (page 58)

Materials used:

• Size 11° seed beads:
    • Transparent orange
    • Transparent light green
    • Transparent sapphire
• Fringes include:
    • Czech molded glass beads
    • Oval Italian millefiori beads
    • Guatemalan clay parrot
• Size 6° transparent light green seed beads for strap
• Half a yard of three-quarter inch light green ribbon

This project is a flattened tube with the bottom stitched together.

To create the body of the purse. String 80 seed beads and tie into a circle. Allow a one-quarter inch space between the last bead and the knot. Place the circle over a support. See Lightweight Supports for Beading (page 7).

Take the needle and thread through the first bead. Pick up three seed beads and pass through bead five of the circle of beads (figure 1). Thread on three more beads and pass the needle through the fourth bead to the left of the last bead worked, bead nine (figure 1). Continue adding new beads in groups of three and connecting at each fourth bead of the base strand until you reach the end of the circle.

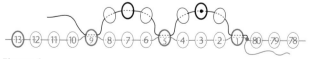

Figure 1

At this point, go back through bead one, which now contains three threads, and up through the next two beads of the first three-bead loop of row two (figure 2). This step-up will be done at the end of each row. Continue creating rows until the tube is two inches high.

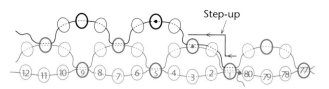

Figure 2

> **Note:** *The dotted bead is the last bead of the step-up and the place where the next row starts.*

To add accent beads. Near the bottom, bring the needle up a few rows and out through one of the connector beads. Pick up an accent bead, run the needle through the next connector bead to the left (figure 3). Continue around until you've finished.

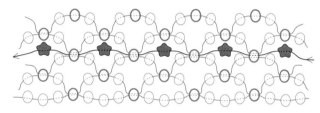

Figure 3

To attach the ribbon to the top rim. Measure the circumference of the tube at its widest. The lattice netting stitch is quite flexible so be sure to stretch the netting before measuring. Cut three-quarter inch ribbon the length of the circumference plus a generous seam allowance. Fold the ribbon in half along its length. Iron the seam flat. Remove the tube from the support. Leave a seam allowance and begin stitching the inside of the folded ribbon to the top of the loops (figure 4a). Use a thread of the same color as the ribbon.

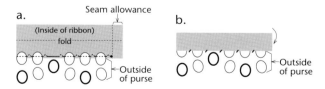

Figure 4a & b

After the ribbon is attached to the inside body of the purse, seam and trim the ribbon. Fold the ribbon forward and carefully tack the front edge of the ribbon to the back edge of the ribbon (figure 4b).

To apply edge beading to the ribbon. After the ribbon is stitched to the top of the purse, you may want to add a row of edge beading to the top of the ribbon. Figures 5a and b show two alternatives.

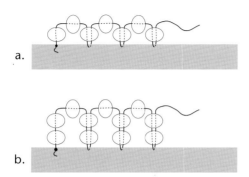

Figure 5a & b

To close the purse. Flatten the tube so the seam of the ribbon is on one side. Align the center beads of each bottom loop and stitch closed (figure 6).

Figure 6. The gray beads represent the connector beads and are for clarity only.

To make the fringe. Select the beads for the long, straight fringes. Remember, these straight fringes are longer in the middle of the purse. Zig-zag in a new thread if needed and exit the first connector bead used to "zipper" the purse closed. Working from right to left, string enough seed beads and focal beads for the first fringe. In order to hang a pendant or bead at the bottom of a fringe, create a small circle of beads before doubling back (see Fringe, page 51).

After attaching the first fringe, bring the needle back through the beads to the next connector bead used to "zipper" the purse closed. Create the next fringe. Continue across the bottom, hanging a fringe from each connector bead.

To make the branched fringe. See Branched Fringe on page 51. Choose a color or combination of colors for the branched fringe. Bring the needle out a few beads above the long fringes and string 14 seed beads. Skip the last bead and pass back through the next three seed beads. String four seed beads and return through all but the last bead — a branch. Continue up the original strand for four more beads and repeat the branch. Pass back through the last six beads of the original 14. Carry the thread through a few beads on the bottom of the purse and make another branched fringe. Continue to make these fringes until the bottom of the purse resembles the canopy of a tropical rain forest.

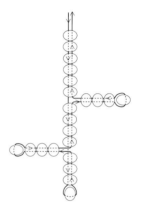

Figure 7

To make the strap. Think of the strap as a necklace. Decide the ideal length. String on a size 6° green seed bead, approximately six inches of size 11° orange seed beads and then another size 6° green seed bead. Continue stringing size 11° orange seed beads with an intermittent size 6° green seed beads until the strap is the desired length. End with a size 6° green seed bead. Be sure to have at least 20 inches of thread on each end of the strands for finishing the strap.

Take a second strand through the first size 6° green seed bead. String enough size 11° green seed beads to match the initial section of size 11° orange seed beads in the first strand. Pass the needle through the next size 6° green bead and again string enough size 11° green seed beads to match the next section of the first strand. Continue stringing and connecting the second strand until you pass through the last size 6° green seed bead.

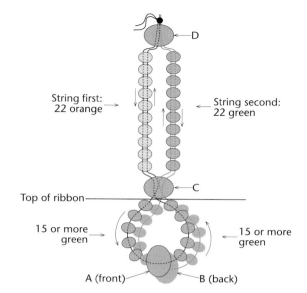

Figure 8. *Illustration does not represent the actual bead count.*

Near the top of the purse, close to the bottom of the ribbon, stitch two size 6° green seed beads to the front (bead A) and two to the back (bead B) of the purse (see the photograph, page 16). To a tail of the orange strand string 22 size 11° orange seed beads, one size 6° green seed bead (bead C) and then another 15 size 11° green seed beads (figure 8). Take the needle through the size 6° green seed bead you've attached near the top front of the purse (bead A). Check to see that bead C on the strap sits above the ribbon. If not, add more size 11° green seed beads. Pick up 15 or more size 11° green seed beads and pass back through bead C. Continue up the strand of 22 orange and exit bead D.

Repeat this procedure with the other tail using size 11° green seed beads. You should now have two tails exiting the top of bead D. Pull the working threads up a little tight and tie together using a surgeon's knot. Make sure the knot is tied around the strand threads. Glue the knot and thread each individual tail up through a strand. Attach the other end of the strap in the same manner.

Rain Forest Medicine Bag

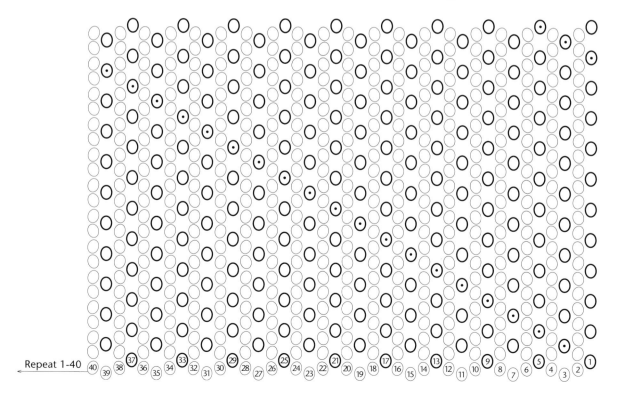

Project Four
The Basket Bag

Carol Wilcox Wells

Carol Wilcox Wells is a graphic artist who finds her inspiration everywhere. The blue of a robin's egg against the brown mud of the forest floor. The color combinations in a piece of fabric. In fact, Carol says she has so many ideas, she can't do them all. As she tells her students, "Look around you for your next design."

Sections to be read before beginning:

- Tubular Peyote Stitch — Even-Count (page 46)
- Branched Fringe (page 51)
- Threads, Knots and Bead Graphs (page 52)
  - To begin tubular peyote stitch (page 53)
  - How to read even-count tubular peyote graphs (page 57)

Materials used:

- Miyuki delica beads:
  - DB-10
  - DB-310
  - DB-324
  - DB-351
  - DB-380
- Size 13° white Czech charlottes for the branched fringe.
- Olive and black satin cord (1 yard each)
- Fray Check™

This four-sided basket involves a series of reductions to create a flat bottom.

> **Note:** Since there are four identical sides to this unusual basket bag, the graph on page 23 describes only one-quarter of the total number of beads in each row. Repeat the pattern four times to complete each individual row.

To begin. String 96 white beads. Tie the beads into a circle, allowing a four bead space between the knot and the last bead. Slip the circle over a support. See Lightweight Supports for Beading (page 7). Working from right to left, pick up the first bead of row three, the dotted bead. Continue row three and make the appropriate step-up (figure A-11, page 46). The dotted bead on the graph indicates the first bead of each row. Continue beading until row 39 is finished.

To reduce for the flat bottom. Slide the beaded tube up the support until the edge is level with the row to be worked. Be sure to have plenty of thread on the needle. Remember, there are four point A's on the bottom which become the corners of the purse. The reduction begins at any point A on figure 1 and the graph. Take the needle and thread above the single black bead as if you were adding a bead, but do not include one. Continue beading the row until the next corner (point A) and reduce again. Reduce at each of the four corners of the row.

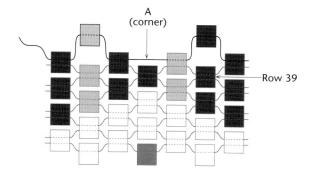

Figure 1

If you do not decrease at each of the four corners, the bottom will become slightly skewed (figure 2). Since the bottom will be covered with branched fringe, this is not critical.

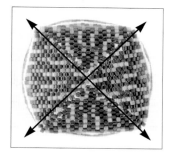

Figure 2

> **Work Tip:** Rather than skipping the bead at point A to span the gap, use a size 14° seed bead to reduce in each corner of each row. This can allow for a more uniform reduction.

Continue doing the tubular peyote stitch for several rows without making a reduction. Exactly where to do a reduction will depend on the size of the seed beads and the stitch tension of your woven work. This technique is not as difficult as it may appear. Periodically decrease at each corner as the space gets smaller. Although the space may seem a bit big as you skip a bead, this gap will close a little with the next row. As you work, gently fold the beading over the opening of the support. Continue to peyote with a reduction from time-to-time until the bottom is closed. Zig-zag the thread through a few beads, half-hitch around the woven thread, pass through a few more beads and clip.

To make the branched fringe. Begin a new thread and exit one of the center beads. Stitch longer branched fringes to the center of the flat bottom and then gradually smaller fringes as you cluster the fringes along the four reduction seams. Follow the arrows on figure 2. Do not cover the entire bottom.

String 20 white charlottes. Without returning through the last bead, pass back through four seed beads and exit. String four white charlottes and one pink or green delica, double-back through all but the colored bead and exit. You've just created a branch. We did not put a colored delica on every branch. Continue up the original strand for seven more beads and exit. Make another branch and finally pass back through the last eight beads of the original 20. Re-enter the anchor bead on the bottom from the opposite side. Otherwise the fringe will flop over (figure 3).

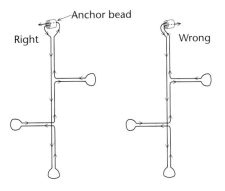

Figure 3

Carry the thread through a few beads along an axis and create another branched fringe. Continue to bead new fringes, gradually decreasing the number of beads in the original strand and the branches, ending with nine beads in the strand and three beads in the branches. To help keep the thread from snagging, cover the fringes you've already done with your hand.

To make the netted top. At the top of the beaded tube, zig-zag in a new thread and exit any of the upper beads of the top rim. String three white delicas, one pink delica and three more white delicas. Take the needle through the fourth uppermost bead to the left of the start (figure 4).

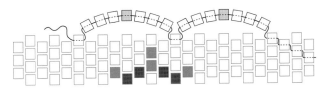

Figure 4

Continue until you meet the beginning loop. Re-enter the first connector bead and back through the first four delicas, exiting the pink delica. String three white delicas, one green delica and three white delicas. Pass through the pink delica of the lower loop (figure 5). String the next loop and converge through the pink bead of the lower loop. Alternate between rows with a pink center bead and rows with a green center bead until you've completed nine rows.

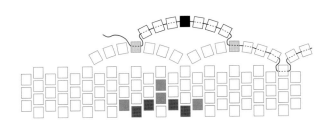

Figure 5

To make the strap. Decide where you would like the purse to hang on your body. Measure the distance and cut two times the length of satin cord plus 14 inches of both olive and black. Fold each in half and loop together as shown in figure 6. Flatten the netting.

Beginning at one side, thread one half of the olive cord to the other side through the front portion of the netting. Turn the bag over and from the same side thread the other half of the olive cord through the back side of the netting. Pull some cording through and loosely tie the two strands together with an overhand knot about three inches from the end. Beginning from the opposite side and one netting hole below, repeat with the black cord.

Check to see if the length is still suitable. Adjust if necessary and tighten the overhand knots. Knot each cord end and trim close to the knot. Cover with Fray Check™. After it has dried, randomly sew delicas over the outer end of the knot to conceal the cord ends.

Figure 6

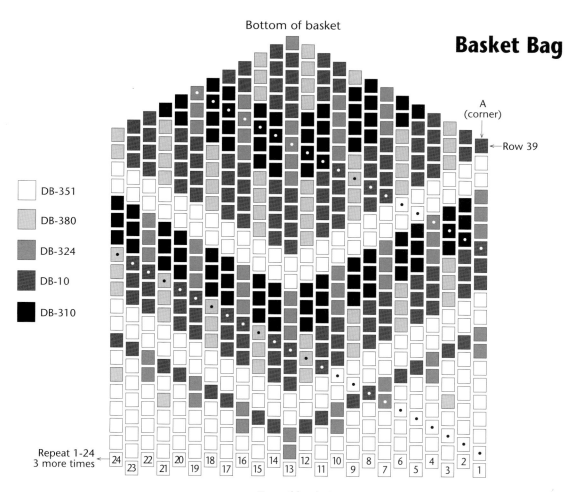

Basket Bag

Bottom of basket

A
(corner)

← Row 39

DB-351

DB-380

DB-324

DB-10

DB-310

Repeat 1-24
3 more times →

24 23 22 21 20 19 18 17 16 15 14 13 12 11 10 9 8 7 6 5 4 3 2 1

Top of basket

Project Five
Golden Elegance

Yoshie Nakashin and Yoko Hiroe

This project was created by the design team of the Japanese bead manufacturing company Miyuki Shoji Co. Ltd. Yoshie Nakashin and Yoko Hiroe make the new samples and draw the designs. Beadwork is designed for the use of the members of the Delica Bead Loom Association in Japan, which has about 2,500 members in four levels of membership.

Sections to be read before beginning:

- Threads, Knots and Bead Graphs (page 52)
  - To begin loomed bead weaving (page 53)
  - How to read loomed bead weaving graphs (page 57)

Materials used:

- Miyuki delica beads:
  - DB-34 round gold
  - DB-41 silver-lined clear
  - DB-36 cut silver
  - DB-34 cut gold
- Small crystal drop
- Two 4mm gold-filled beads
- Loom of your choice

This purse is loomed as one hour glass shaped piece. The warps are then pulled up to close the bottom.

Note: This project is not for beginners and presumes you are already familiar with loomed bead weaving.

The heart-shape bottom of this purse is unusual for a loomed bag. The purse is loomed in one piece and then the warp threads are pulled up through the work to close most of the purse and create the rounded bottom. Therefore, the small hourglass graph represents the shape of the finished loomwork (page 29). Graph one depicts the front of the purse, graph two depicts the back and graph three the flap.

To begin. Attach 34 warp threads at least eighteen inches long to your loom. The finished loomwork is 5 1/2 inches long, plus you will need at least six inches on both ends to be able to weave the warps into the body of the loomwork.

To weave the bag. About three inches down from the center of the loom, tie the weft thread around the seventh warp thread from the left, leaving a four-inch tail.

Work Tip: While looming, be sure not to pierce any of the warp threads because to complete this purse, you must be able to pull the warps up after weaving the beads. To ensure that the needle crosses above the warp threads, push the beads up between the warps until the silver glint of the needle is clearly visible as it crosses above the warp threads.

String on 21 round gold delicas and take the needle and thread under the center warp threads. Push the beads up between the warp threads and bring the needle up through the sixth space from the right. Pass through the beads from right to left. There should be six gaps between the warp threads on both sides of the loomed beads.

String on the 23 beads of row two, take the thread over the top of the sixth warp thread from the left and then below the center warp threads and loom as before (figure 1). Add a bead to each end of rows three through seven to gradually increase the loomwork to the full width of the warp threads.

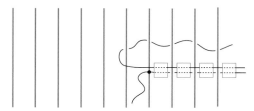

Figure 1

To reduce. Upon completing row 10, take the needle under the last warp thread and back through the first bead of row 10. This will lock the bead in place and put the weft thread in position to begin row 11 (figure 2). When reducing, do not pull the weft thread too tightly or the outer bead will be pulled out of line.

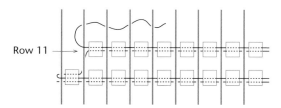

Row 11 →

Figure 2

For each reduction, use extra care not to pierce a warp thread when going through the last bead of the previous row. Continue to bead up the graph and reduce from both sides until only one bead is left. Do not repeat this last bead. You have just finished looming the front of the purse and the single bead of the bottom. Continue to graph two. The next row of three beads begins the back of the purse.

Be sure to pull the warp threads close to the woven beads as you begin decreasing the back portion of the bag. You may have to move these warp threads in closer to weave them in snugly. Upon reaching the top of graph two, the main body of the purse is complete and the weaving should resemble an hourglass.

To weave the flap. String the beads of the first row of the flap on graph three and take the needle over both the seventh and sixth warp thread (figure 3). Then take the beads under the warp threads and loom as usual. Weave as per graph three.

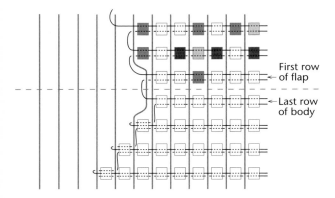

Figure 3

To finish. Now that all the weaving is done, remove the beadwork from the loom. Fold the loomwork up so the bottom of the purse is the single bead. Holding the loose ends of each warp thread, pull them up until the loops of warp thread at the sides of the bottom are gone and the beads are snug up against each other.

 Note: If a warp thread has been pierced, pull the warp up from whichever end pulls freely.

Zig-zag the individual warp threads of the front and the flap into the beadwork. See points A and B, figure 4.

To close the shoulder of the purse (point C), use a square knot and tie the first outside warp of the front to the first outside warp of the back. Continue tying the remaining four pairs of warp threads on the shoulder. Repeat on other shoulder.

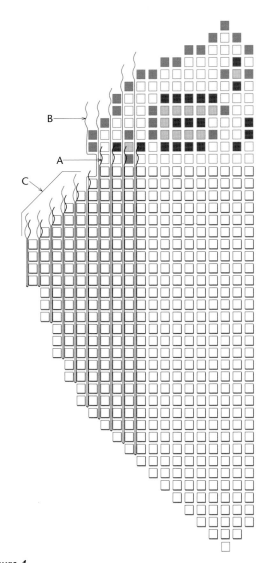

Figure 4

To create the fringe. Take the thread out through the top outside bead of one side of the purse. Do several half-hitches to secure the thread. String the following delicas:

- One cut silver
- Nine round gold
- One cut silver
- One silver-lined clear
- One cut gold
- One cut silver
- Five round gold
- Five cut silver

Run the needle through all but the last five cut silver delicas to create a loop at the bottom of the fringe. Run the needle back through the last two beads of the row, then take the needle down along the next lower row. String the next fringe (figure 5).

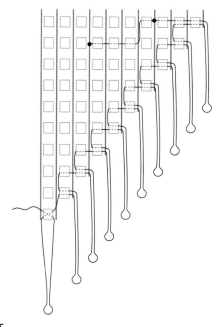

Figure 5

To create the loops on the flap. For the threading path refer to figure 6. For each loop string the following delicas:

- Five round gold
- One cut silver
- One cut gold
- One cut silver
- Five round gold

String the following delicas for the center loop with the crystal drop:

- Seven round gold
- One cut silver
- The crystal drop
- One cut silver
- Seven round gold

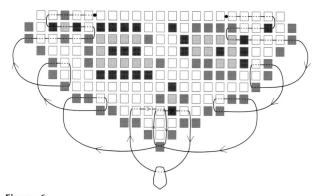

Figure 6

To make the strap. String enough round gold delicas to create the desired length of strap. String a second strand of the same length. Tie the two strands together with a surgeon's knot. Slip a 4mm gold bead onto the tied end. Pass the tails through bead A as shown on graph three. Weave each tail back into the loomwork using several half-hitches to secure the strap.

Twist each strand of the strap tightly. Tie the two strands together with a surgeon's knot. Slip a 4mm gold bead over the two tails. Be sure to keep the twists in each strand while weaving the tails back through bead B and into the loomwork. Use several half-hitches to secure the strap.

Golden Elegance

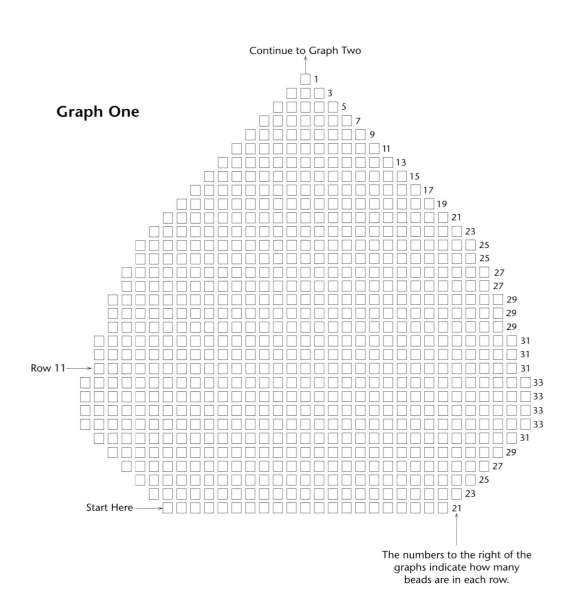

Continue to Graph Two

Graph One

Row 11 →

Start Here →

The numbers to the right of the graphs indicate how many beads are in each row.

Golden Elegance

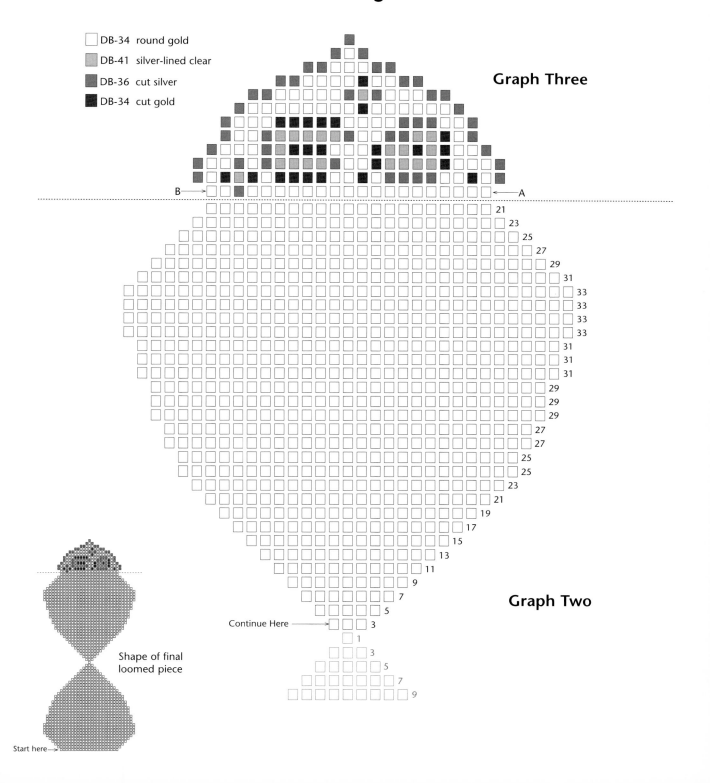

DB-34 round gold
DB-41 silver-lined clear
DB-36 cut silver
DB-34 cut gold

Graph Three

B→   ←A

21
23
25
27
29
31
33
33
33
33
31
31
31
29
29
29
27
27
25
25
23
21
19
17
15
13
11
9
7
5
Continue Here →   3
1
3
5
7
9

Graph Two

Shape of final
loomed piece

Start here→

Project Six
Winged Bag

David Chatt

As a full-time bead artist and educator, David Chatt spends countless hours developing beading techniques. "I think of beadwork as a sculptural medium and set out to develop its three-dimensional capabilities." The single-needle, right-angle weave as described in this book is one of David's developments. He is known primarily for his bead encrusted glass vessels.

Sections to read before beginning:
- Single-needle, Right-angle Weave (page 48)
  - Decreasing at the sides (page 51)
- Threads, Knots and Bead Graphs (page 52)
  - To begin single-needle, right-angle weave (page 55)
  - How to read single-needle, right-angle weave graphs (page 58)

Materials used:
- Size 11° Czech seed beads:
  - Opaque medium red
  - Transparent dark red
  - Opaque medium orange-yellow
  - Transparent orange-yellow of a different tone than the opaque orange-yellow
  - Opaque black
  - Opaque white
- Size 12° transparent yellow three-cut seed beads
- Size 5° or 6° opaque red seed beads
- Two large opaque red oval glass beads
- Four 4mm and four 8mm transparent dark red glass rondels

This purse is formed by sewing a triangle to a square.

Note: We highly recommend making samples if you have not done this technique before. It takes time to become familiar with the threading path of this stitch and to be able to read the graph. This project will require patience the first time.

Note: Both the red and yellow seed beads of this project are several tones of each color hue, which then lends richness and visual interest. Mix the groups of color randomly, don't worry about creating a pattern within the yellow or red areas of the design. However, do be careful not to have too many beads of an individual color together, especially the opaques, because those groupings would detract from the graphic design of the finished purse.

Work Tip: If you need to back-track and redo a square, loosen the square and pull the thread back through the beads and then pull the needle back through the bead.

To begin. Start in the lower left corner of the graph one on page 34, string four seed beads and then pass the needle back through beads number one through four again to make a circle. Tie a knot.

Pick up the three beads of the next square. Take the needle up through the right vertical bead of the first group of four. Pass back through the upper horizontal bead and down through the right vertical bead of the new square (figure 1).

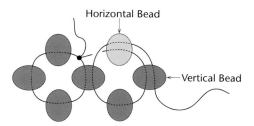

Figure 1. Vertical and horizontal refer to the direction of the hole in relation to the already woven beads.

To begin the third square, pick up three beads. Take the needle down through the right vertical bead of the previous square, across through the lower horizontal bead and up through the right vertical bead (figure 2).

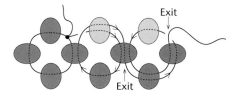

Figure 2

The squares will alternate between a counter clock-wise and clock-wise threading path. Think in terms of turning corners, every time you come through a bead — turn a corner. Never take the thread across an open space to another bead. By continually turning corners, the beads are pulled into the characteristic right-angle weave pattern. Periodically look at the interstices of the bead squares to make sure the threading path is correct (figure 3).

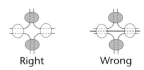

Right   Wrong

Figure 3

Continue beading row one following the graph. Upon completing the last square of row one (figure 4), take the needle through the upper horizontal bead. Thread the three beads of the first square of the second row and once more take the needle back through the upper horizontal bead of the last square of row one and the left vertical bead of the new square. Turn the work around and begin again from right to left.

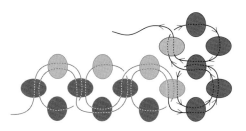

Figure 4

From now on, only the first square of each row will require three beads. Subsequent squares will require only two new beads (figure 5). Each new square will be formed from the two new beads plus the upper horizontal bead of the previous row and the closest vertical bead of the last square of the current row.

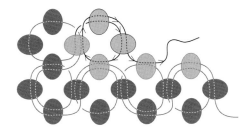

Figure 5

Continue beading the rows as indicated on the graph. Be careful not to miss any squares or the work will not lie flat and the beadwork will be skewed.

To bead the triangular front portion, begin on the bottom left corner of graph two on page 35 and work from left to right. Reduce as indicated.

To decrease at a side. After picking up the two beads of the last square of the row, take the working thread down through the right vertical bead of the previous square, the lower horizontal bead, the left vertical and the upper horizontal bead of that same previous square. (figure 6). Begin beading the new row. Following the graph, complete beading the triangular front portion.

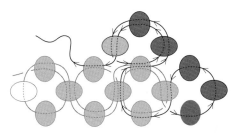

Figure 6

Attach the triangle to the square. Turn the square on the diagonal and lay the triangle over the top of the square, following the faint gray outline on graph one. Using large stitches placed 1/2 inch from the edge, temporarily sew the triangle in place. To permanently secure the triangle, choose a bead two or three beads from the edge and attach it to a bead of the square. Be sure to thread through the beads, never around the woven threads of the square or the triangle. After the triangle is attached, remove the temporary stitching.

To add the fringes to the edges. Add two-bead fringes between the outside seed beads on the two long sides of the triangle and all four edges of the square. See the photograph on page 30. Bring a new working thread out between any one of the outer edge seed beads, string two size 11° seed beads and double back through the first of the two beads (figure 7). Take the needle through the next outer bead of the netting and string a size 6° and then a size 11° seed bead. Double back through the size 6° seed bead and pass through the next outer bead of the netting. Continue alternating the fringes around the perimeter of the square and both long sides of the triangle. After frilling the edges, you might want to go around again to add an even more textural quality to your work.

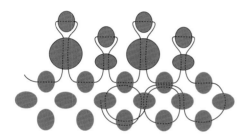

Figure 7

To make the strap. Decide the ideal length for you. Temporarily tie one end of two strings around a stop bead, take both strings through a smaller and then a larger red rondel, a large red oval focal bead, a larger rondel and a smaller rondel. With only one of the strings add an 11°, a 6°, an 11°, a 6°, etc. to complete the desired length of strap. Add the final two rondels, a large red oval focal bead and the last two rondels. Temporarily tie the string around another stop bead. Allow generous tails on both ends of the strand.

Take the second working thread through the first size 6° seed bead, create a size 11° two-bead fringe (figure 8). Pass through the next size 6° and begin a two-bead fringe. Alternate both sizes of fringe along the full length of the strap. Take the thread through the second set of rondels and focal bead. Untie the stop bead and tie the two strands together with a surgeon's knot. Attach both tails of one end of the strap to the purse using several half-hitches to support the weight. Repeat on the other end of the strap.

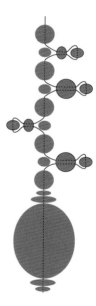

Figure 8. *Illustration shows thread path for strap fringe and does not show initial thread.*

Winged Bag

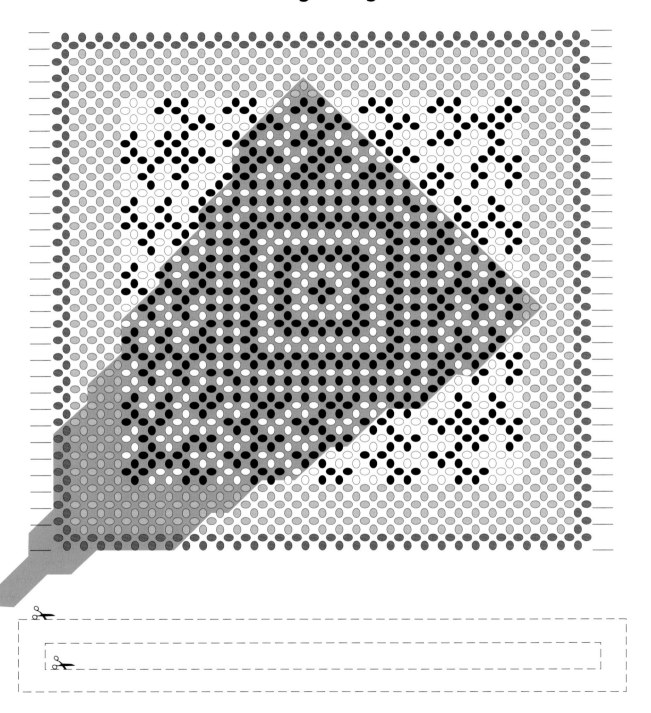

Graph One

Winged Bag

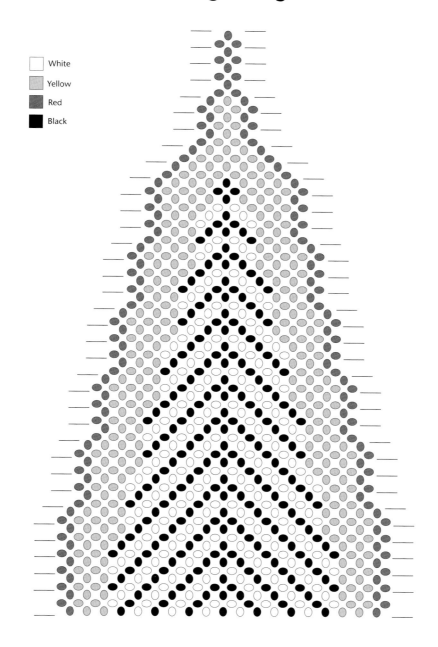

White
Yellow
Red
Black

Graph Two

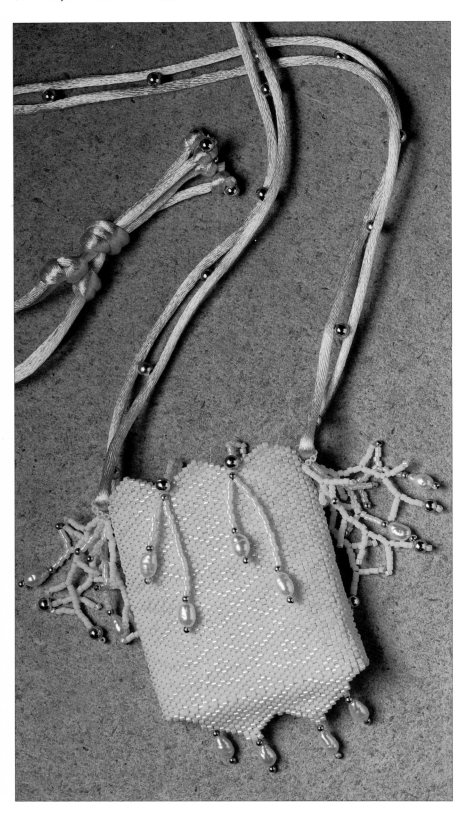

Project Seven
Damask

Carol Wilcox Wells

Carol Wilcox Wells considers herself lucky to have discovered art early. Her working experience as a graphic designer has taught her to work backwards. As a design or pattern comes to mind, she does a quick sketch of the final project. Because Carol uses peyote stitch almost exclusively, she always graphs the specifics to mathematically figure out where to begin. Sometimes, a solution is readily apparent, other times the design rests in her mind and presents itself later.

Sections to read before beginning:

- Tubular Peyote Stitch — Even-Count (page 46)
- Flat Peyote Stitch — Even-Count and Odd-Count Decreasing at the sides (pages 44 and 45)
- Fringe (page 51)
- Threads, Knots and Bead Graphs (page 52)
    - To begin tubular peyote stitch (page 53)
    - How to read even-count tubular peyote graphs (page 57)

Materials used:

- Miyuki delicas:
    - DB-352 bone white
    - DB-203 pearlized bone white
- 46 2mm round gold-filled beads
- 36 4mm round gold-filled beads
- 16 freshwater pearls
- Cream satin cord (2 1/2 yards)
- Fray Check™

This match-box shaped purse is created by adding a flat bottom to a tube.

> *Work tip: The edges of metal beads can be sharp and therefore could cut your thread. Use a small file and smooth the edges of the hole. Small jewelry files are called broaches.*

To Begin. Following the bead pattern of the graph on page 41, string 88 seed beads to form rows one and two. Tie the thread into a circle. Allow a four-bead space between the knot and the last bead, otherwise the peyote stitch will be too tight. This space will be taken up when you add row three. Place the circle of beads over a support. See Lightweight Supports for Beading, page 7.

Be sure the pattern, beginning with bead number one, is to the left of the knot. Working from right to left, take the needle through bead one. Pick up the dotted bead and peyote stitch the beads of row three.

> *Work Tip: This white on white project can be difficult to follow. In the initial rows, you might want to lay out the beads in order first and then peyote stitch the beads for each row.*

Follow the graph and complete the main portion of the purse. Ignore the X's on the two beads in row two of the graph. The X's indicate these beads are anchor beads which will each hold one of the two-fringe embellishments on the front of the purse.

Upon completing the last row of the main portion of the graph, take the thread over to bead A on the upper right corner of the graph. Pass through bead A with the needle pointing toward bead B.

> *Note: The X's on row 73 indicate the anchor row for both the flat bottom and the front and back bottom flaps.*

To stitch the flat bottom. Starting at point A, use the odd-count flat peyote stitch to bead the seven row rectangle of the flat bottom. Bead only one rectangle. This panel will be folded over and attached to the other side of the purse to create the flat bottom. The flat bottom is not visible in the photograph on page 36 because the front triangular flaps obscure it.

After completing the seventh row of the panel, fold the flap over the opening toward the back portion of the tube. Line up the top right bead of the extension with the space to the left of bead A on the other side and "zipper" the bottom closed (figure 1).

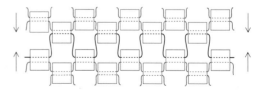

Figure 1. The gray-lined beads are for clarity only and do not represent beads in the project.

Once the back is properly aligned and "zippered" closed, stitch the sides of the bottom closed. Sew from left to right and then right to left. Take the working thread through the first lower bead of the tube and then through the side bead of the flat bottom (figure 2a). Continue closing the side. Reverse direction and then take the needle back through the upper beads of the tube and the side beads of the bottom flap (figure 2b). Repeat this procedure to close the second side of the bottom.

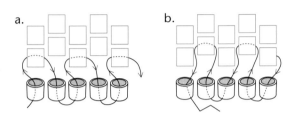

Figure 2a & b

> **Note:** *The photograph on page 36 shows only one bottom flap on this purse, the other is tucked behind the bag.*

To make the bottom flaps. Each panel is worked using the odd-count flat peyote stitch. Start with plenty of thread. Zig-zag through the woven beads and exit bead A from the left. The first row of the flap will also start from row 73. Stitch row one of the flap as indicated on the graph. Exit through bead B. Half-hitch around the left woven thread and pass back through bead B and the last bead of row one. You are now ready to bead row two. Continue beading the rows. As appropriate, either half-hitch around the woven thread between the beads or around the edge thread at the beginning and end of each row.

To add the flap pendants. Upon completing row eight, the thread will have exited bead I (figure 3). Pick up bead J, the first bead of row nine, and then add a 2mm gold bead, a freshwater pearl and another 2mm gold bead. Return through the freshwater pearl and the first 2mm gold bead. Pass the needle back through bead J and around through bead I. Pass through J again and all the pendant beads again for extra strength. Take the thread through beads J and I again and lastly through bead K. Pick up the second bead of the row (bead L) and continue.

Finish row nine with a second pendant added to the last bead of the row. From now on the flap diverges into two separate triangles. As per the graph, complete these triangles with a another flap pendant hanging from each apex.

Bead a second flap to the other side of the bottom in the same manner. The first row of the flap will begin with bead A on the opposite side.

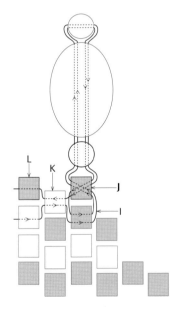

Figure 3

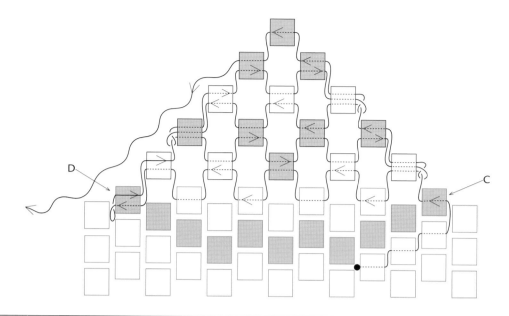

Figure 4

To make the triangular points at the top of the purse. Decide which is the front of the purse and which is the back. Place the triangular points on the front first.

Turn the beaded tube over and read from the graph in figure 6. These points are done one at a time (figure 4). Zig-zag through the body of the purse and exit bead C from the left. Follow figure 4 and peyote stitch the next five beads. Exit bead D. Half-hitch around a woven thread to secure the row and pass the needle back through bead D and the last bead of the row. Continue adding rows and reducing until there is only one bead left.

After anchoring the single bead at the top, zig-zag the thread down through the beads and out through bead X (figure 6) and make the first fringe embellishment.

String:
- One 2mm gold bead
- 20 pearlized delicas
- One 2mm gold bead
- One fresh-water pearl
- One 2mm gold bead

Return the needle through all but the bottom bead. Be sure to snug the fringe up against the beadwork. Take the needle into the woven beads. Bring the needle again through the first 2mm gold bead.

String:
- 10 pearlized delicas
- One 2mm gold bead
- One fresh-water pearl
- One 2mm gold bead

Return through all but the bottom bead including the first 2mm gold bead and back into the woven beadwork.

Zig-zag over to bead E and make the next triangular point. Hang the second two-strand branched fringe from the other bead X. Make the third triangular point beginning at bead G.

Upon completing the third triangle, take the thread through the woven beadwork and exit bead H. Using the odd-count flat peyote stitch, make the first of the cord conduits.

To secure the button. On the front of the purse, zig-zag a new thread entering bead D from the right. Pick up a 4mm gold bead and take the needle through bead E (figure 6). Half-hitch around a woven thread. For added strength, return through bead E, the gold bead and bead D. Half-hitch again. Pass back through bead D, the gold bead and bead E. Add second button between beads F and G.

To make the triangular points on the back. Zig-zag a new thread through the woven beads and exit bead C of the back. Bead the first triangular point as per the front. Take the thread through the woven beads and exit bead D. To make the button loop, string 16 bone white delicas and pass the needle through bead E and half-hitch (figure 5). Double back through the loop for added strength and exit bead D and half-hitch again. Return through the loop and bead E. Beads F and G indicate the first and last anchor beads of the second button loop.

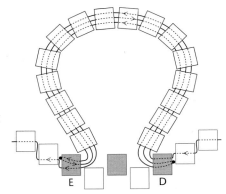

Figure 5

Create the next triangular point, the second loop, the third triangular point and the second cord conduit.

To finish the cord conduits. Zig-zag a new knotted thread into the beadwork and exit bead H. Roll down and stitch the extension to the outside of the purse. See the photograph on page 36.

Add five branched fringes to the base of the conduit. String 29 bone white delicas, a 2mm gold bead and a pearlized delica. Return through the gold bead creating five, small, bone white branches as you go up the strand. Place a pearlized delica at the tip of each branch.

Carry the thread over a bead and create the second branched fringe. String 29 pearlized delicas, a 2mm gold bead, a freshwater pearl, and another 2mm gold bead. Take the thread back up six or seven pearlized delicas and exit. String on four or five pearlilzed delicas for a branch. Place a 2mm gold bead at the tip of each branch. Alternate between a bone white fringe and pearlized fringe.

To make the strap. Decide the ideal length of strap. Cut two pieces of cord twice the finished length plus 12 inches. Thread a cord through each conduit. Be careful not to snag it on the beads. Center each cord in the conduit. Close to the conduit, sew a 4mm gold bead between the two strands of cord. The gold bead looks like a bridge between the two strands.

Divide the total length of your finished strap by 24 and use that measurement to space the gold beads. Take the needle through the cord and exit where you want the next gold bead. Sew a total of 12 gold beads between the two strands of each side.

Using an overhand knot tie the four ends of the cord together. Tie a tight overhand knot to the end of each individual cord strand. Trim the ends and apply Fray Check™. After it dries, sew a 4mm gold bead to each of the four ends.

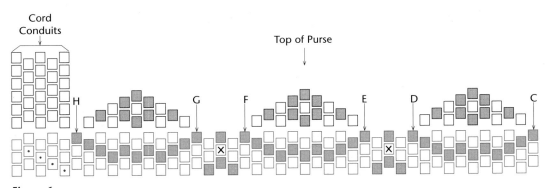

Figure 6

Damask

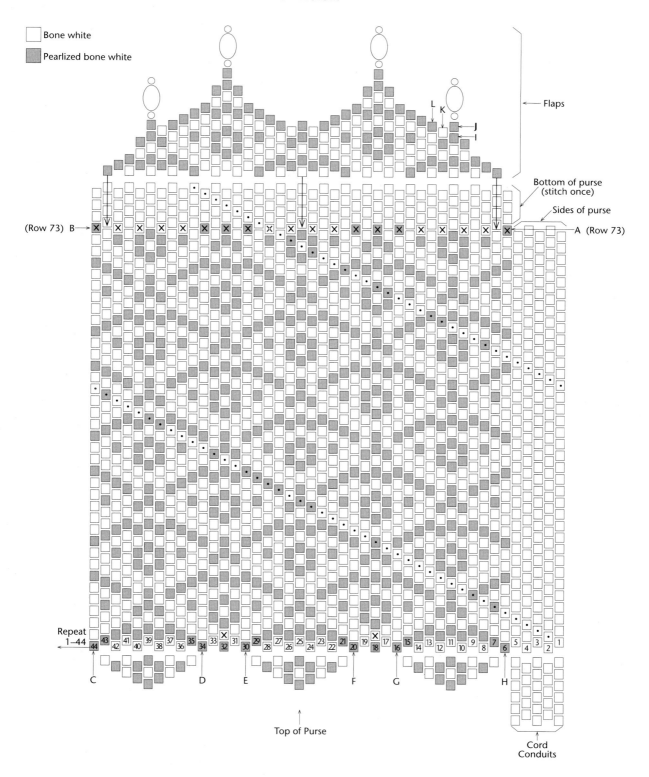

□ Bone white

■ Pearlized bone white

Flaps

L K J I

(Row 73) B

Bottom of purse
(stitch once)

Sides of purse

A (Row 73)

Repeat
1–44

44 43 42 41 40 39 38 37 36 35 34 33 32 31 30 29 28 27 26 25 24 23 22 21 20 19 18 17 16 15 14 13 12 11 10 9 8 7 6 5 4 3 2 1

C   D   E   F   G   H

Top of Purse

Cord
Conduits

Glossary

Anchor bead. A designated bead in the fabric of the bead weaving through which a fringe is attached.

Base strand. The first string of beads from which the remainder of the bead weaving develops. In the peyote stitch, this base strand of beads includes both rows one and two. See figures B-11, B-12 and B-13 on pages 56, 57 and 58.

Connector bead. In the lattice netting weave, one of many recurring beads that link the adjacent rows together. In the straps of Projects One, Two, Three and Seven, the connector bead is a focal bead (defined below) which periodically joins two separate strands.

Edge thread. The selvage edge of the woven beadwork. The series of outside thread loops which naturally develop as the beading moves back and forth from one row to the next. See figure A-1b, page 43.

Focal bead. A bead that acts as a prominent design element in a particular composition.

Horizontal bead. The upper or lower bead of a square created by the stitch pattern of the single-needle, right-angle weave. The hole of the bead is horizontal to the woven beadwork. See figure A-21a, page 50.

Step-up. A threading procedure to join the beginning and end of a row in even-count tubular peyote stitch or lattice netting stitch that results in a straight row and then enables the start of a new row. See figures A-11a & b and A-13, pages 46 and 47.

Stop bead. A miscellaneous bead used to hold the thread and beads of the base strand in place at the beginning of the bead-weaving. The stop bead ensures even tension initially when weaving flat peyote. After a few rows, this bead is untied and the thread is worked back into the woven fabric of the beading. See figures B-3a & b, page 53.

Vertical bead. The right or left bead of a square created by the stitch pattern of the single-needle, right-angle weave. The hole of the bead is vertical to the woven beadwork. See figure A-21a, page 50.

Warp. The multiple parallel threads attached to a bead loom in loomed bead weaving. Warps may be individual threads tied at each end of the loom or one continuous thread running back and forth from one end of the loom to the other. There will always be one more warp thread than the number of beads in the widest portion of the loomed piece.

Weft. The working thread that secures the beads between the warp threads in loomed bead weaving. First the weft is strung with the beads of a row and then passed under the perpendicular warp threads. Then, each bead is pushed up between two adjacent warp threads. The weft thread is again passed through the beads, this time above the warp threads. The beads are held in place by capturing the warp threads between the lower and upper path of the weft thread.

Working thread. The thread on the needle actively linking the beads into a woven fabric or a strand of beads. See figure A-1b, page 43.

Woven thread. The thread in bead fabric which links the beads together and holds the beads in place. See figure A-1b, page 43.

Zig-zag. The path used to secure a thread at the beginning or end of beadwork. The thread is passed back and forth by making several short alternating turns. This zig-zag threading pattern can secure the beginning or end of a thread without a knot or glue. See figure B-2, page 53.

Appendix A
Beading Techniques

The purses of this book were created using one or more of the following beading techniques: tubular peyote, odd-count flat peyote, tubular lattice netting, loomed bead weaving and single-needle, right-angle weave. If you are unfamiliar with any of these techniques, we strongly recommend making samples. Consider using much larger beads to make the early samples. The even-count tubular peyote and the odd-count flat peyote are innovative variations on the more conventional peyote stitches. The single-needle, right-angle weave is an especially unusual and initially challenging stitch. Expect the first few rows of all these off-loom techniques to be unruly in appearance and awkward to stitch. The work should even out after the third or fourth row.

This book has been written for right-handers because, unfortunately, we have not developed the coping skills that left-handers have mastered. We apologize to our left-handed readers.

Flat Peyote Stitch — Even Count

This variation on the flat peyote stitch uses an even number of beads in the base strand. An even-count peyote graph will always have the left edge bead in the base row higher than the edge bead on the right side of the graphed pattern. In figure A-1, bead one is higher than bead eight. This is the more conventional peyote stitch which always has a place readily available for the first bead of each new row.

For a sample. Temporarily secure a stop bead to the end of the thread leaving a 4-inch tail (see figure B-3, page 53). String eight large seed beads. Size 6° works well, but any larger sized seed beads will do. To make it easier to see rows one and two as they develop, alternate between a dark and a light bead in this base strand (figure A-1a). Working from right to left, pick up a light bead, bead nine, and pass the needle back through bead seven. Pick up another light bead and this time pass back through bead five. Continue across the base strand as indicated in figure A-1b.

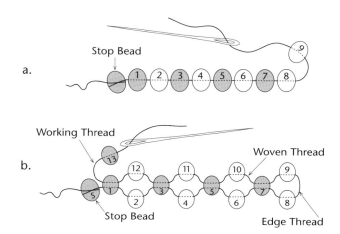

Figure A-1a & b. The thread gaps were drawn to make the threading pattern more apparent, but are not visible in the finished work.

As the beads are put into place for row three, each alternate bead in the base strand is pulled up, thus creating a first and second row. Although stringing both rows one and two at the same time may be confusing, they are now readily apparent after adding row three.

To begin the fourth row, turn the work around and work from right to left again. Pick up a dark bead, bead 13, and pass the needle down through bead 12. Continue adding dark beads to complete row four (figure A-2). Repeat rows three and four until you're comfortable with the stitch.

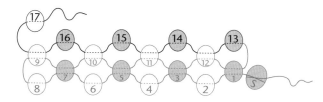

Figure A-2

Flat Peyote Stitch — Even-Count

Decreasing at the sides

Continuing with the sample, put the needle under the edge thread from left to right — the needle will be pointing away from the woven beads. Pull the thread through. Take the thread over both the edge thread and the working thread to create a loop. Above the loop, pass the needle under the working and edge thread. Pull the thread up and tug gently. This half-hitch secures the working thread around the edge thread (figure A-3). Double-back through bead A and then through bead B. Continue beading the row.

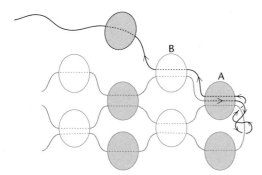

Figure A-3

To reduce the other side, turn the work around and repeat the same reduction to the next row (figure A-4). To reduce the next row, half-hitch onto a working thread between beads B and C. All following reductions will anchor in the same manner.

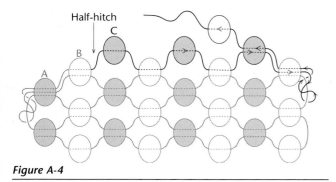

Figure A-4

> **Note:** *It is not possible to reduce symmetrically from both sides in even-count peyote or end with a single, centered bead. If a design calls for a symmetrical reduction culminating in a single bead, use odd-count flat peyote.*

Flat Peyote Stitch — Odd-count

Used in Projects Two and Seven

This method of reducing is used on the triangular flap of Project Two, and on the bottom front and back flaps of Project Seven.

In order to center the geometric design in Project Two, the artist used the less conventional odd-count peyote stitch to create the body of the purse. The base strand consists of an odd number of beads. You can always recognize an odd-count beading pattern by the lower outside beads of row one. Note beads one and nine of figure A-5b. Do not graph an odd-count flat peyote pattern with the edge beads higher in row one. It is very difficult to begin row three.

To make a sample. Temporarily secure a stop bead to the end of the thread leaving a 4-inch tail (see figure B-3, page 53). String 9 large seed beads. Size 6° works well, but any larger sized seed bead will do. Alternate between a light and a dark bead in the base strand (figure A-5a). Working from right to left, pick up a light bead and pass the needle back through bead eight (figure A-5b). Pick up another light bead and this time pass the needle back through bead six. Continue across the base strand as indicated.

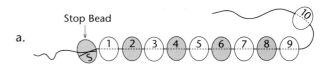

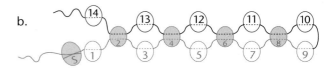

Figure A-5a & b

Upon reaching the the end of row three and exiting bead two, there will be no last bead to put the needle through and make the turn to begin row four.

To hold the last bead of row three in place, you will need to do a figure eight threading pattern (figure A-6a). Take the needle down and through bead one from left to right. Pass through bead two and then down through bead three. Reverse direction and take the needle up and through bead 13, again through bead two and down through bead one. Pass the needle around the edge thread and back through bead 14, the last bead of row three. You are now ready to begin row four.

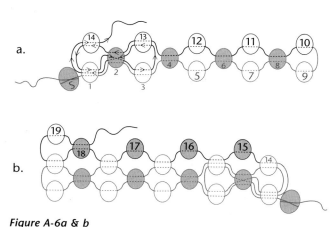

Figure A-6a & b

At the end of row four and all even numbered rows, the turn will be the same as in even-count flat peyote and will not require any adjustment (figure A-6b). Upon reaching the end of row five and all subsequent odd-numbered rows, pick up the last bead of row five and take the needle down to the edge thread between rows one and three. Do a half-hitch around the edge thread and then pass back through the last bead of row five (figure A-7). Repeat rows three and four until you're comfortable with the stitch.

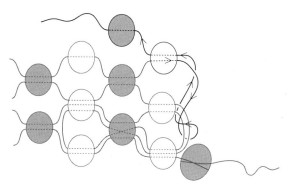

Figure A-7

Flat Peyote Stitch — Odd-Count

Decreasing at the sides

Used in Projects Two and Seven

To decrease at the sides in odd-count flat peyote stitch, simply stop one bead short at the end of the row. In order to avoid threads looping around the outside beads, do a half-hitch as in figure A-8 and continue beading the row. As you return, you will be doing an even-count peyote stitch.

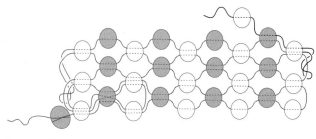

Figure A-8

Upon reaching the other side, half-hitch around a woven thread between beads A and B as shown in figure A-9. Continue reducing in this same manner until only a single bead is left. Zig-zag down through the beadwork and clip.

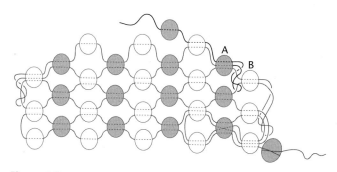

Figure A-9

Tubular Peyote Stitch — Even-Count

Used in Projects One, Four and Seven

Historically, tubular peyote stitch is woven with an odd number of beads in the base row which results in a continuous spiral bead path. However, the purses in this book use an even number of beads in the base strand. This even-count tubular peyote stitch results in a straight top and bottom after flattening the tube. The bottom can then be stitched closed to create the body of the purse. The even-count stitch also allows for a centered, symmetrical design in the finished beadwork. A centered design such as Project One or circular, symmetrical geometric design such as Project Four will always be an even-count pattern.

To make a sample. String 30 large seed beads. Size 10° works well for this sample. Alternate between dark and light beads in this base strand. Tie the beads into a circle. Between the knot and the last bead allow a space equivalent to one or two beads (figure A-10). Otherwise the tension of the first three rows will be too tight. This space will be taken up when you do the third row. Place the circle of beads over a support. See Lightweight Supports for Beading, page 7.

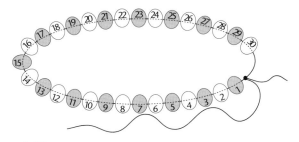

Figure A-10

Note: If the graphed design immediately begins with a bead pattern in the first two rows, you will need to check for a correct or incorrect placement of the circle of beads on the support. Place the circle so the first beads to the left of the knot are the first beads, at the bottom right on the graph — numbers 1,2,3, etc. If not, either take the circle of beads off the support and flip the circle or slide the circle down to the other end of the support.

To begin row three. Working from right to left, take the needle through the first bead to the left of the knot. Pick up a light bead and put the needle through bead three of the base strand. Pick up another light bead and pass through bead five (figure A-11a). Continue beading the circle until you meet bead one.

Pick up the last bead of row three and pass back through bead one (figure A-11b). Thread again through the first bead of row three, the dotted bead.

Note: The dotted bead indicates the first bead of each row in even-count tubular peyote stitch. For further information, see "How to read tubular peyote stitch graphs" on page 57.

You have just done a step-up. Rows one, two and three are now complete and the top of the work is straight. A step-up joins the beginning and end of a row and is now required at the end of each subsequent row. Pick up the next dotted bead to begin row four. Continue beading the rows of even-count tubular peyote stitch until you've mastered them. From time-to-time slide the woven beads down the tube.

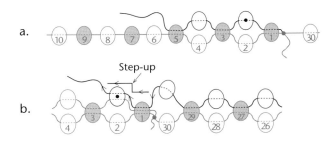

Figure A-11a & b

Work Tip: The tension of the first three rows may still not equal the tension of the latter rows. This is not unusual. It's not always easy to gauge how long a thread space to leave between the knot and the circle of beads in the base strand. If the tension is uneven, undo the first three rows and reweave them after the beaded tube is complete. Or bead the first three rows in a different color and then begin the first row of the graphed pattern after the surrogate three rows. Undo these three rows after the tube is completed.

Tubular Lattice Netting

Used in Project Three

Tubular lattice netting results in an open-work bead fabric. A new row is woven by taking the needle through a bead of the previous row at regular intervals. This technique is usually worked over multiples of four, so the total number of beads in the base strand should be at least 40 and divisible by four.

To make a sample. String a dark bead then three light beads. Repeating this combination, pick up a total of 40 beads. Allow a one-quarter inch space between the last bead and the knot. Tie into a circle. Place the circle over a support (see Lightweight Supports for Beading, page 7). Working from right to left, take the needle through the dark first bead to the left of the knot. Pick up a light, a dark and a light bead and take the needle through the fourth bead to the left of the knot — a dark bead. Again pick up a light, a dark and a light bead and go through the next dark bead to the left of the last connector bead (figure A-12). Continue beading around the base strand.

When you reach the knot, it is time to do the step-up and merge the beginning and end of the row. Take the needle back through the first bead to the left of the knot and up through the first two beads in the group of three that began row two (figure A-13). You should have exited the dark middle bead. This second pass through the connector bead of the base strand and the first two beads of the row is the step-up.

To begin row three. Pick up a light, a dark and a light bead and again take the needle back through the next dark middle bead of the loop of the previous row (figure A-13). Try practicing using a single color until you're sure of the stitch.

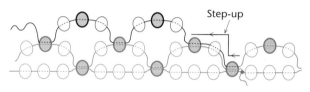

Figure A-13

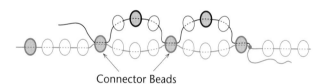

Connector Beads

Figure A-12

Single-needle, Right-angle Weave

Used in Project Six

In this technique, a series of squares or cells are formed to create a netting. The beads lie at right angles to each other. Regular graph paper is excellent for plotting the squares of this stitch. This stitch may be initially difficult to learn so David Chatt, the artist of Project Six, recommends learning the stitch using a 12 bead unit first then learning the 4 bead unit.

To make a sample. String 12 beads and tie into a circle. Do not make the circle too snug because you will need to backtrack through three of the beads. Try to think of this circle of beads as a square with three beads on each of the four sides (figure A-14a). Working from left to right, pick up nine beads. Pass the needle back through the three right vertical beads of the first square, exiting before the knot (figure A-14b). Take the needle again through the first six beads of the second square, exiting at the opposite corner from the knot. The new square has nine new beads which uses three beads of the previous square to make the fourth side.

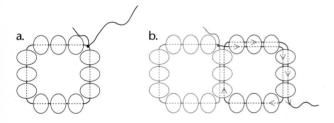

Figure A-14a & b

String nine more beads and return the needle down through the right three vertical beads of the last square. Pass the needle back through the lower three horizontal beads and the right three vertical beads of the new square (figure A-15). You should have just exited the opposite corner from the exit point of the last square. This stitch alternates between a counter-clockwise and a clock-wise threading pattern.

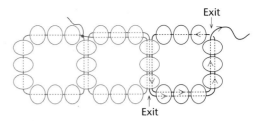

Figure A-15

Note: With the exception of the last square, the needle will always exit a completed square, alternating between exiting the bottom and exiting the top. To begin a new row, the final exit point in the last square will depend upon whether there are an even number or an odd number of squares in the row.

The sample has an even number of squares in each row. Continue to make squares by adding nine new beads to each square. Complete nine squares. The threading path of the final and tenth square of the row will differ from the previous squares.

To bead the last square of a row with an even number of squares, pick up another nine beads and pass the needle through the vertical beads of the last square and then through the upper horizontal beads. Stop here. Usually, you would also pass down through the right vertical beads of the new square. You are now in position to begin a new row (figure A-16).

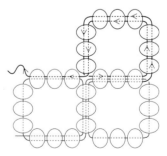

Figure A-16. *Starting a new row with an even number of squares per row.*

Note: To complete the final square of a row with an odd number of squares, exit the last square as usual at the top of the right vertical beads. Take the needle back through the upper horizontal beads of the last square. You are now in position to begin a new row (figure A-17).

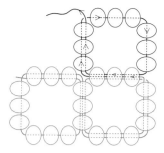

Figure A-17. Starting a new row with an odd number of squares per row.

To continue with the sample and begin row two, string on nine beads and pass the needle through the upper three horizontal beads of the last square of the previous row and then pass through all nine new beads of the square again (figure A-16).

For the next square, pass through the three upper horizontal beads of the second to the last square of the previous row and string on only six beads. Take the needle down through the three right vertical beads of the last square, across through the three upper horizontal beads of the lower square and finally up through the left vertical beads of the new square.

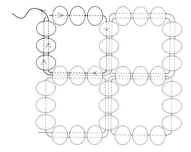

Figure A-18

From now on, with the exception of the first square of each row, pick up only six beads to make each new square. The threading pattern always turns a corner. As the thread is pulled around the corners, the beads take on the characteristic right-angle weave bead pattern. Never take the thread across any open space between squares.

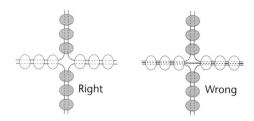

Figure A-19. The example to the left is done correctly. The example to the right illustrates an error.

It may appear that making continual circles without turning the corners of the counter-clockwise and clock-wise threading pattern would create the same effect. The following photograph illustrates the difference.

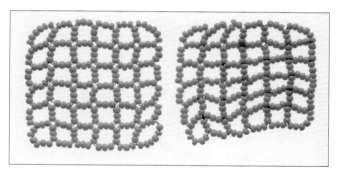

Figure A-20. The sample on the left is the single-needle, right-angle weave.

Practice this beading pattern until you can anticipate the next threading path of each new square. It becomes second nature sooner than you might think. We recommend making a new sample with only four beads per square and becoming proficient at the single-needle, right-angle weave before attempting Project Six. Not only will you be working with an unfamiliar stitch but you will also have to keep track of an initially challenging color bead pattern.

To begin the new sample. String four beads and tie into a snug circle (figure 21-a). Working from left to right, begin to add squares. With the knot in the top right corner, pick up three beads and take the needle back up through the right vertical bead of the previous square. Pass back through the upper horizontal bead of the new square and the right vertical bead of the new square in order to position the thread to begin the third square (figure A-21b). You will have just exited through the bottom of the right vertical bead.

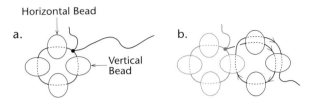

Figure A-21a & b

String on three beads and pass down through the right vertical bead of the last square. Go back through the lower horizontal and the right vertical bead of the new square. You will have just exited through the top of the right vertical bead.

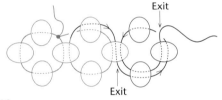

Figure A-22

Make six more squares for a total of nine squares. The thread should have exited through the top of the last vertical bead. In order to turn the corner and be in position to begin a new square take the needle through the upper horizontal bead of the last square (figure A-23). Thread on three beads and pass back through the upper horizontal bead of the last square of the last row and the left vertical bead of the new square.

Figure A-23

Pick up two beads and go back through the upper horizontal bead of the square of the previous row, the left vertical of the previous square, the upper horizontal and the left vertical of the new square and then through the upper horizontal bead of the previous row (figure A-24). The four sides of the square are made up of the two new beads picked up, the upper horizontal bead of the lower square and the left vertical bead of the last square. From now on, pick up three beads for the first square of each row and then pick up only two beads to make each of the following squares of a row.

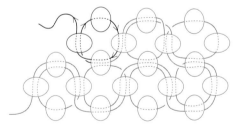

Figure A-24

To make the third square of the second row, string on two beads and pass down through the left vertical bead of the previous square, the upper horizontal bead of the lower square and up through the left vertical bead of the new square (figure A-25).

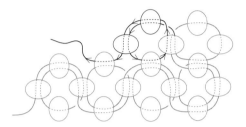

Figure A-25

Continue making squares and starting new rows until you can go through several of the beads in a square without taking the needle out through each bead. Practice until you begin to anticipate the threading path and are able to take these shortcuts.

Single-needle, Right-angle Weave

Decreasing at the sides

Used in Project Six

Decreasing at the sides of the single-needle, right-angle weave is very simple. Be sure you have completed the row and then position the thread to begin one square from the edge.

If the row has an odd number of squares. Add the two beads of the last square, then take the needle down through the left vertical bead of the previous square, through the lower horizontal of the second from the last square of the row, up through the left vertical bead of the same square, and finally through the upper horizontal of that same inside square (figure A-26). You have just gone through all four beads of the second square from the edge. String on three beads and continue as usual.

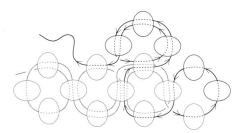

Figure A-26. Decreasing with an odd number of squares per row.

If the row has an even number of squares. When completing the last square of the row, do not pass through the upper horizontal bead as usual. Exit the left vertical bead and then pass through the upper horizontal bead of the previous square of the row (figure A-27). String on three beads and continue as usual.

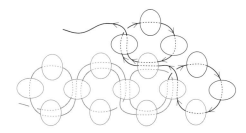

Figure A-27. Decreasing with an even number of squares per row.

Fringe

Fringe adds movement to the woven beadwork. It can also obscure a seam. Fringe is an excellent design element in which to use larger beads that are difficult to incorporate within the woven bead fabric.

To make a single standard fringe element. String several beads. Take the needle back through all but the last bead strung. In other works, the thread goes through the bottom bead only once but twice through all the other beads of the fringe (figure A-28a). Figure A-28b is a variation of this fringe.

Branched Fringe

The branched fringe, or kinky fringe, has become very popular in the last few years and can be surprisingly versatile. In Projects Three and Four, the artists used densely packed, longer branched fringes to lend textural and visual interest. In Project Six, David Chatt used two larger beads to make short branches to create a very textural, frilled edge around the woven bead fabric.

To make a sample of branched fringe. String sixteen seed beads and take the needle back through the first three of the last four beads. Bring the needle out between the fourth and fifth bead from the bottom. String on four beads and take the needle back through three beads — a branch. Continue up the strand passing through four more beads. Make another branch and continue up four beads, make another branch. Exit out the last four beads of the main column (figure A-28c).

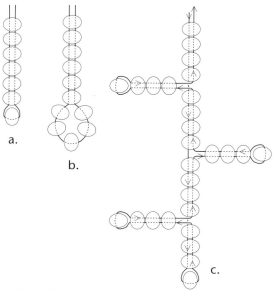

Figure A-28a, b & c

Appendix B
Threads, Knots and Bead Graphs

Threads

We generally recommend starting with 30- to 36-inches of working thread. Wax the thread by pulling it once or twice across a small piece of beeswax. The wax will strengthen the thread and help keep it from tangling and fraying. It also helps prevent piercing the woven threads. If there is a little too much wax on the thread, it will come off on the beads. Don't worry. It wipes off easily.

In general, we recommend a single thread to make these purses. All of the project purses in this book were beaded using a single thread. It creates a more supple piece of beadwork and also allows more passes through each bead. A double thread does offer more strength and more assurance that a knot will stay after it is pulled into a bead. However, the finished amulet purse will be stiffer. The choice of a single or double thread is up to the individual beader.

Knots

Knots should be obscured to allow the beauty of the beading to be appreciated. Some of the methods given below may seem time consuming, but will pay off in the quality appearance of your finished work.

Half-hitch. Used to attach the working thread to the edge thread when decreasing at the side of flat beadwork (page 44). Also used to secure the tails of a working thread to the woven threads while zig-zagging back through the beadwork. A few half-hitches help ensure that the beginning and ending tails do not come out and show through the woven beads.

Square knot. Used to tie an old working thread to a new working thread. Remember — right over left and then left over right makes a neat, tidy and tight knot.

Surgeon's knot. Used to tie the strap to an amulet purse. Pass right over left and right over left again — left over right and left over right again. This knot is especially strong and difficult to undo, so be sure the knot is where you want it before tightening it.

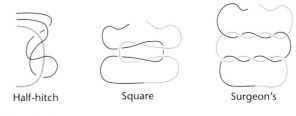

Half-hitch   Square   Surgeon's

Figure B-1

To keep knots from unraveling

We recommend finishing all knots with a bonding agent. Use a small amount of Fray Check™ (available from notions departments), clear nail polish, or Germanow-Simon Hypo-Tube Cement (watch crystal glue). Even though the Hypo-Tube cement has its own one-drop applicator, we recommend using a pin or needle to place a small drop of the glue or nail polish on the knot. Do not let the glue glob over the surrounding beads.

If the thread is nylon based, such as Nymo, you can seal the knot by melting it. Although lighters and matches have been used successfully, we prefer to use an incense stick. It provides an easily managed heat source which gently melts the knot. Melting a knot is only appropriate for the first knot of a new working thread. Do not apply any heat near the beadwork.

Beginning and Ending Threads

To zig-zag

In the off-loom and the loomwork stitches, zig-zag the thread tails back into the bead weaving to secure the beginning or end tails of thread. The threading path will pass through the woven beads in short alternating turns. Be careful not to cross the thread over the top of a bead when turning to make the zig-zags. Pass the needle diagonally through several beads, half-hitch the tail around a woven thread. Reverse direction and again take the needle through several beads, half-hitch around a woven thread. Reverse direction for the last time and take the needle through a few more beads. Clip the tail and seal the knots.

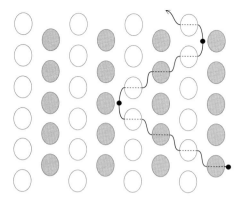

Figure B-2. The illustration shows a peyote stitch sample.

> **Work Tip:** *If the old working thread is too short to weave back in with the needle attached, put your needle into the beadwork and then thread the eye of the needle with the short tail. Repeat. Try to avoid this situation, it's awkward to do.*

To begin flat peyote stitch

To start the base strand of flat peyote stitch, temporarily tie a stop bead to one end of the working thread, leaving about a four-inch tail. This bead helps hold the base strand in place. Use a knot that is easy to untie since it will be removed after a few rows are completed. String the beads of the base strand. Complete several rows of the peyote design and then untie the stop bead. Thread the tail on the needle and do a couple of half-hitches around the edge thread to secure the first bead of the base strand (figure B-3a). Take the needle back through the beading and zig-zag through the beads of the weaving. When using a double thread, tie the tails together around the edge thread with a square knot and zig-zag each tail back into the bead weaving (figure B-3b).

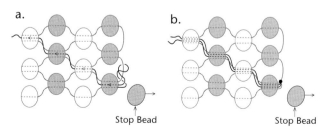

Figure B-3a & b

To begin tubular peyote stitch

Tie the base strand into a circle of beads. For every twenty-five beads of the base strand, allow approximately a one bead space between the last bead and the knot. Otherwise, the tension will be too tight. This space will be taken up when the third row is completed. After a few rows have been woven, zig-zag the tail with a few intermittent half-hitches into the woven beads. Glue the knots.

To join a new working thread. Be sure to have at least four inches of thread left on the old working thread. Tie a knot to one end of the new working thread and zig-zag through the woven beads. Gently tug the knot into a bead. Plan the zig-zag path so the needle exits the same side of the last bead as the old working thread. Using a square knot, tie the new and the old working threads together as close to the last bead as possible. Complete a few more rows and then zig-zag the tail of the old working thread back into the woven beadwork (figure B-4). Glue the knot after completing a few rows.

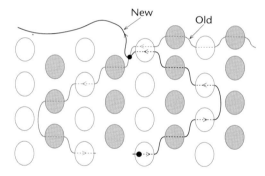

Figure B-4.

To begin loomed bead weaving

After warping the loom, tie a weft thread around the left edge warp. Be sure to leave at least a four-inch tail. After looming a few rows, zig-zag the beginning tail through the loomwork. To do this, weave back through part of the first row (figure B-5). Carry the tail up to the next row, reverse direction and pass through a few beads and then repeat with a third row. Clip the tail at the back of the loomwork. Take care not to clip a warp or a weft thread.

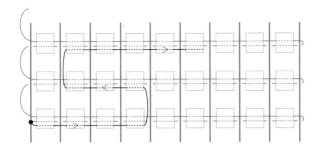

Figure B-5

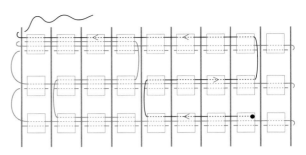

Figure B-7

To join a new working thread. Start a new thread if there isn't enough working thread to complete another row and weave the thread back into the loomwork. Always begin a new working thread at the edge of the loomwork.

To end the old working thread and lock the current row in place, take the needle under the warp thread. Guide the needle back through several beads of the row, carry the needle down to another row and reverse direction. Pass the needle through a few more beads, then down to another row and reverse direction again for a few more beads (figure B-6). Clip the thread, do not clip a warp or weft thread.

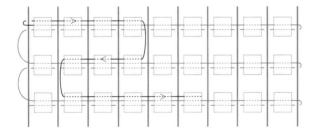

Figure B-6

To begin the new working thread, tie a knot in the end of the new working thread and zig-zag through two or three rows taking the needle through the last six or seven beads of the last row (figure B-7). Gently pull the knot into a bead and commence looming.

As an alternative, tie the new working thread around an interior warp thread and run the tail back through a few beads and clip. Bring the working thread through the beads to the edge of the weaving and begin the next row.

Note: This method of tying a weft thread to a warp thread is not appropriate for Project Five because the warp threads then cannot be drawn up to create the rounded bottom of the amulet purse.

To begin tubular lattice netting

Netting stitches are inherently loose, we advise using knots to secure the working threads in place. Tie the base strand into a circle of beads. For every seventy-five beads, allow approximately a 1/4" space between the last bead and the knot. Otherwise the base row will be tight and the sides of the netted tube will flare out as you stitch the bottom of the purse closed. After completing several rows, zig-zag the four-inch tail up through the woven beads.

To join a new working thread. Zig-zag through the beadwork and exit the last bead. Use a square knot to tie the old working thread and the new working thread. Complete a few more rows and then zig-zag the old thread back through the woven beads (figure B-8). Clip the thread in the back of the work. Glue the knots.

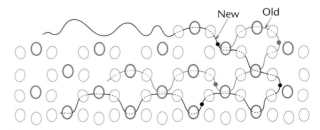

Figure B-8

To begin single-needle, right-angle weave

Tie the base strand into a circle of beads. After several rows of beading, return the tail back through the bead-work, do not cross any open areas between the squares. Pass through several beads, half-hitch the tail around a woven thread, carry the tail through a few more beads, half-hitch again and take the needle through a few more beads (figure B-9). Clip the tail, taking care not to cut a woven thread then glue the knots. If you wish to avoid knots, take the thread around through the beads of one or two squares again.

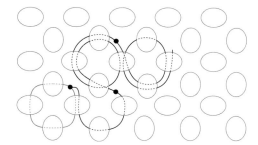

Figure B-9

To join a new working thread. Follow the beading path of two squares and exit the same bead as the old working thread. Use a square knot to tie the new working thread to the old working thread (figure 10a). Pick up the appropriate number of beads and complete the next square. After working several rows, take the tail of the old working thread and circle back through the beads of one or two squares (figure 10b). Take care to never cross an open space in the netting.

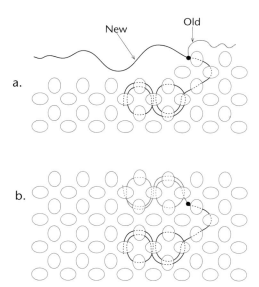

Figure B-10a & b

Bead Graphs:
How to Use Them

With the increased interest in designing original seed bead artwork and the widespread use of computers, we now have many beadwork graph papers available which reflect the one-side-longer-than-the-other ratio of seed beads. We don't have to contend with the distortion caused by using the standard square ratio graph paper. These new beadwork graph papers are available for sizes 10° to 22° in the peyote stitch, the netting stitch, the right-angle weave, the brick stitch and the herringbone weave.

To make the graphs in this book easier to use, we recommend photocopying the graph of the project and coloring the beads of the photocopy.

©**Copyright:** This permission to photocopy is for your own use only.

Tape the photocopied graph to a board or table. You will need a guide to isolate the beads of each row. Choose a guide which is thin, does not have a distracting design and is wider than the graph.

Use Post-it™ correction tape (available from office supply stores) to hold the guide in place and then reposition the guide as you work up the rows of the graph. Or tape the graph to a metal surface and use a magnetic strip as a guide.

How to read flat peyote stitch graphs

Working from left to right, consecutively pick up all the beads of the base strand (rows one and two) beginning with bead one of figure B-11. Then read row three from right to left. If the bead pattern is symmetrical, it is not necessary to alternate from one direction to the other when reading the graph.

Upon reaching the end of a row, move the guide upward a half a bead and reverse direction on the graph. Pick up the beads indicated by the whole beads below the guide (Figure B-11).

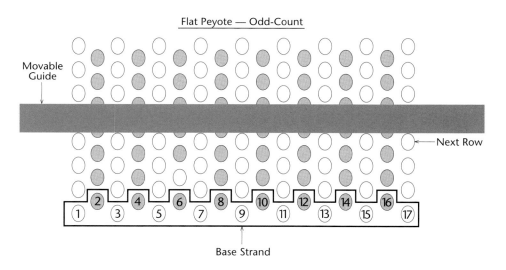

Figure B-11

How to read even-count tubular peyote graphs

The tubular peyote graphs in this book show only one side of the finished purse: the other sides are identical to the side graphed. Consecutively pick up all the beads of the base strand (rows one and two), beginning with bead one of figure B-12. Pick up all the beads of the base row again when making Projects One or Seven. For a total number of beads double that of the first two rows of the graph. Project Four requires picking up the beads of the base strand four times to create the four-sided basket for a total of four times the number of beads shown on the graph.

The dotted bead indicates the first bead of each row in even-count tubular peyote stitch. With each new row, the first bead is one bead to the left of the first bead of the previous row.

Note: The dotted beads on the graph form a diagonal line going from right to left up the graph. Upon reaching the edge bead of the left side, the next dotted bead will be the first bead of the next row on the right edge of the graph (Figure B-12).

Move the guide up only half a bead at a time. The new whole beads immediately below the guide are the beads of the current row.

How to read loomed bead weaving graphs

Loomed bead weaving graphs are read from left to right. After beading a row, the new row will always begin on the left side of the warp threads.

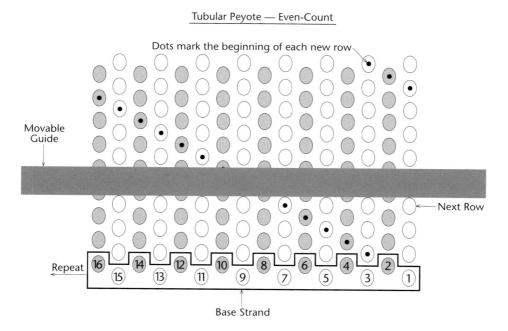

Tubular Peyote — Even-Count

Figure B-12

How to read tubular lattice netting graphs

Tubular lattice netting graphs are read from right to left. The tubular graph shows only one side of the finished tube. Be sure to pick up all the beads of the base strand twice for a total of double the number of beads indicated in the base strand of the graph (figure B-13).

Tubular lattice netting requires a step-up to complete a row and position the tread to begin a new row. The beads drawn with a heavier lines are the connector beads. The dotted connector beads indicate the last bead of the step-up and the starting place for each new row.

Place the guide above the row being stitched. The upper connector bead beneath the guide (bold outline) is the center bead of each three-bead loop in the current row.

How to read single-needle, right-angle weave graphs

The graph of this stitch is not read one row at a time like the other stitches described in this book but involves reading three rows of beads to create each new row of squares. Furthermore, the beads are not picked up in a linear fashion but as a series of clockwise and counter clockwise circles.

The graph is much easier to use with the guide we have provided (page 34). Photocopy it onto index paper or card stock and cut out along the lines. Always have three rows of beads showing in the rectangular opening of the guide (figure B-14). With the exception of the first row of squares, the bottom row is composed of the upper horizontal beads of the previous row of squares. The top two rows represent the new beads being worked.

The lines at the edges of the graph indicate which rows are worked as a unit. For the first unit of beading, pick up the bottom three rows on the graph. After the first three rows, move the guide up two rows for each new series of squares. Use a Post-it™ note to help guide you across a row. It's easy to lose your place.

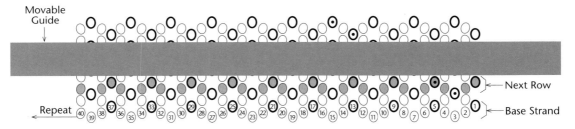

Figure B-13

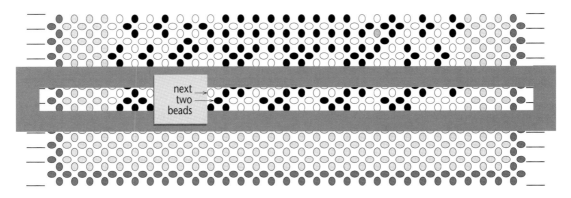

Figure B-14

Beaded Amulet Purses

Gallery

A Gallery of Beaded Amulet Purses

What is a beaded amulet purse? It is an art form...a container... an accessory...an artifact...even a spiritual vessel. Within these palm-sized objects there are no limits. True, they are all containers worn on the chest. Yet, the variety, both emotionally and stylistically, is dramatic. One is abundant in beads and fringe. Another is tightly controlled through pattern and technique. There are no rules here.

Many of the artists who created these wonderful pieces have advanced degrees in other fine arts and "found their milieu" in beadwork. Some have been beading for decades, others for merely a year or two. They find obvious joy in stretching the boundaries of the medium and making a personal statement through design, texture, color and technique. The Gallery displays a mere sampling of the current work in this field. It is by no means a comprehensive survey. In the past ten years the field has exploded. New techniques and styles are created every day.

It's not surprising that beaded amulet purses are experiencing a renaissance of sorts. The recent surge of interest in beading accounts for part of it, but beaded bags also have historical touchstones for us. In the seventeenth century when beaded purses first appeared in Europe, they were an essential craft of the well-bred woman. The designs were taken from embroidery patterns and often incorporated legends or symbols. By the nineteenth century, beaded purses became widespread and were mass produced.

Today, we resonate with beaded amulet purses for several reasons. Amulets, tangible symbols of our belief in spirit, cross all cultures. Often, they are contained in small pouches worn over our heart. These bags hold our treasures. Eventually, the pouches themselves become our amulets. We weave together our special stories and symbols. The bags are mystical and mysterious. Nearly every bag is a container. What do they hold? One bag can hold our special beach finds. Another contains one simple stone. They are unified by beauty. We wear them as statements of who we are and how we want to be seen.

Let these gallery pages serve as a source of inspiration. Absorb the artistry, appreciate the personal statement of these artists and launch your own journey. Your personal choice of color, texture, technique and pattern will create your own statement. Ultimately, that is the vision of this book and the joy we find in beadwork.

— Mardie Rhodes

Northern Lights, 1992
Cynthia Rutledge

Silver Art Deco Pouch, 1993
Judy Miner

Spirit Bag, 1990
Anita Parish

Trust, 1993
Jenny Norton

Gilded Cage, 1993
Carol Wilcox Wells

Untitled, 1994
Jennifer Clement

Untitled, 1994
Fran Stone

Twice in a Blue Moon, 1994
Wendy Hubick

Picket Fences, 1993
Susan Jackson

Queen Isabella, 1993
Margo Field

Cave Painting, 1993
Kate Boyan

Primitive Fetishes, 1993
Linda Chapman

Flying Shaman, 1993
Mary Hicklin

The Other Side of the Garden Wall, 1993–1994
Carol Perrenoud

Purple Bag, 1993
David Chatt

Tour My Garden, 1993
Susan Jackson

Untitled, 1993
Judy Miner

Neptune's Beard, 1993
Susan Jackson

Out of the Blues and Amethyst, 1994
Wendy Hubick

Serenity, 1993
Nancy Male

Harlequin Pouch, 1993
Colleen Willmer

Bear, 1993
Sig Wynne-Evans

Untitled, 1993
Linda Chapman

Japanese Sea, 1991
Carol Wilcox Wells

Kokopelli Spirit Pouch, 1993
Margaret Bernard

The Old One, 1993
Cynthia Rutledge

Beagle Dog, 1994
Yoshie Nakashin and Yoko Hiroe